PSYCHOLOGY

Reading and Activity Workbook

Contents

Chapter 1: What is Psychology?

Guided Reading Activities

Chapter 2: Psychological Methods

Guided Reading Activities

Chapter 3: Biology and Behavior

Guided Reading Activities

Chapter 4: Sensation and Perception

Guided Reading Activities

Chapter 5: Consciousness

Guided Reading Activities

Chapter 6: Learning

Guided Reading Activities

Chapter 7: Memory

Guided Reading Activities

Chapter 8: Thinking and Language

Guided Reading Activities

Chapter 9: Intelligence

Guided Reading Activities

Reading and Activity Workbook

Chapter 10: Infancy and Childhood

Guided Reading Activities

Chapter 11: Adolescence

Guided Reading Activities

Chapter 12: Adulthood

Guided Reading Activities

Chapter 13: Motivation and Emotion

Guided Reading Activities

Chapter 14: Theories of Personality

Guided Reading Activities

Chapter 15: Psychological Tests

Guided Reading Activities

Chapter 16: Gender Roles

Guided Reading Activities

Chapter 17: Stress and Health

Guided Reading Activities

Chapter 18: Psychological Disorders

Guided Reading Activities

Chapter 19: Methods of Therapy

Guided Reading Activities

Chapter 20: Social Cognition

Guided Reading Activities

Chapter 21: Social Interaction

Guided Reading Activities

What Is Psychology?   Guided Reading

READING THE SECTION
DIRECTIONS Read each of the following descriptions, and write who or what is "speaking" in the space provided.

_____ 1. "I am the field of psychology that deals with evaluating psychological problems, such as anxiety or depression, and helping people overcome them."

_____ 2. "I am the field of psychology concerned with the changes that occur throughout a person's life span."

_____ 3. "I am the field of psychology that focuses on conducting research through experiments."

_____ 4. "I am the field of psychology dedicated to identifying and helping students who have problems that interfere with learning."

_____ 5. "I am the field of psychology that helps mainly people who have adjustment problems."

DIRECTIONS Read the definitions below. In the space provided, write the letter of the term that matches each definition.

_____ 6. branch of psychology that focuses on patients who are struggling with disabilities

_____ 7. branch of psychology that deals with people and work

_____ 8. branch of psychology that studies social systems that promote and foster individual well-being for members of a community

_____ 9. branch of psychology that examines the relationships between behavior and physical health

_____ 10. branch of psychology that focuses on behavior and mental processes under different cultural conditions

a. health psychology

b. industrial psychology

c. cross-cultural psychology

d. rehabilitation psychology

e. community psychology

POST-READING QUICK CHECK

DIRECTIONS On the line provided before each statement, write **T** if a statement is true and **F** if a statement is false. If the statement is false, write the correct term on the line after each sentence that makes the sentence a true statement.

_____ 11. A <u>psychologist</u> is a medical doctor who specializes in the treatment of psychological problems and can prescribe medication for clients.

_____

_____ 12. A <u>developmental</u> psychologist works within the criminal justice system.

_____

_____ 13. <u>Personality</u> psychologists identify human characteristics, or traits.

_____

_____ 14. <u>Geriatrics</u> is the branch of medicine that focuses on the diseases and problems of the elderly.

_____

_____ 15. Research that has no immediate application and is done for its own sake is called <u>basic</u> research.

_____

DIRECTIONS Write three words or phrases to describe each term given.

16. clinical psychology _____

17. educational psychology _____

18. social psychology _____

19. developmental psychology _____

20. counseling psychology _____

What Is Psychology?

Guided Reading

Section 3

READING THE SECTION

DIRECTIONS Read each sentence and fill in the blank with the correct word or phrase.

1. Some psychologists believe that _____, or looking within, is one way to learn about ourselves. **(gestalt/introspection)**

2. The field of _____ is based on the discovery of the basic elements of consciousness. **(stream of consciousness/structuralism)**

3. The school of thought called _____ emphasizes the importance of unconscious motives and internal conflicts in determining human behavior. **(functionalism/psychoanalysis)**

4. _____ is the scientific study of observable behavior. **(Behaviorism/Observationism)**

5. _____ psychology is based on the idea that our perceptions of objects are more than the sums of their parts. **(Gestalt/Reinforcement)**

DIRECTIONS Read each of the following descriptions, and write who or what is "speaking" in the space provided.

_____ 6. "I concluded that people learn to behave in certain ways because they have received positive reinforcement for their behavior."

_____ 7. "I founded psychoanalysis and the theory of psychodynamic thinking."

_____ 8. "I disagreed with the structuralists and argued that experience is a constant stream of consciousness."

_____ 9. "I lived in ancient Greece and outlined the laws of associationism."

_____ 10. "I asserted that psychology was a science and must be limited to observable, measurable events, an assertion that led me to found behaviorism."

POST-READING QUICK CHECK

DIRECTIONS Look at each set of four terms. On the line provided, write the letter of the term that does not relate to the others.

_____ 11. a. Sigmund Freud
        b. structuralism
        c. psychoanalysis
        d. psychodynamic thinking

_____ 13. a. stream of consciousness
        b. William James
        c. functionalism
        d. Gestalt psychology

_____ 12. a. learning
        b. associationism
        c. Aristotle
        d. Middle Ages

_____ 14. a. reward
        b. B. F. Skinner
        c. introspection
        d. reinforcement

DIRECTIONS Use vocabulary terms to write a summary of what you learned in the section.

_____

_____

_____

_____

_____

What Is Psychology?

READING THE SECTION
DIRECTIONS Read the definitions below. In the space provided, write the letter of the term that matches each definition.

_____ 1. emphasizes the role that thoughts play in determining behavior

_____ 2. emphasizes the effects of experience on behavior

_____ 3. emphasizes the influence of biology on human behavior

_____ 4. emphasizes the influences of ethnicity, gender, culture, and socio-economic status on behavior and mental processes

_____ 5. emphasizes the influence of unconscious forces on human behavior

a. psychoanalytic perspective

b. sociocultural perspective

c. cognitive perspective

d. biological perspective

e. learning perspective

DIRECTIONS In the space provided, write the vocabulary term that best matches each description.

_____ 6. psychological perspective that stresses the capacity for human self-fulfillment and the importance of consciousness, self-awareness, and the capacity to make choices

_____ 7. a group of people who share a common religion, color, or national origin

_____ 8. psychological perspective that focuses on the interaction of biological processes, psychological dispositions, and social factors

_____ 9. theory that suggests people can change their environments and that people can learn intentionally by observing others

_____ 10. psychological perspective that focuses on the evolution of behavior and mental processes

POST-READING QUICK CHECK

DIRECTIONS On the line provided before each statement, write **T** if a statement is true and **F** if a statement is false. If the statement is false, write the correct term on the line after each sentence that makes the sentence a true statement.

_____ 11. Psychologists of the <u>humanistic</u> perspective assume that mental processes are made possible by the nervous system.

_____

_____ 12. <u>Cognitive</u> psychologists study mental processes to understand human nature.

_____

_____ 13. The <u>evolutionary</u> perspective is rooted in the ideas of Sigmund Freud.

_____

_____ 14. Members of <u>ethnic groups</u> are united by their common heritage, race, language, or common history.

_____

_____ 15. The <u>learning</u> perspective stresses the effects of ethnicity, culture, gender, and culture on behavior and mental processes.

_____

DIRECTIONS Answer the questions on the lines provided.

16. What do humanistic psychologists consider the most important aspect of psychology?

_____

_____

17. From where do evolutionary psychologists believe people get their behavior patterns?

_____

_____

What Is Psychology?   Applying What You've Learned

Lab

Public Perceptions of Psychology

What perceptions—and misperceptions—do people have about the field of psychology?

1. INTRODUCTION

First, read through the lab in your textbook. Then use this worksheet to help you complete the lab in your textbook.

2. PARTICIPANT SELECTION

Before you begin to administer your survey, use the chart below to record information about the participants you have chosen. At the bottom of each column of the chart, predict how much you think each person will know about psychology based on his or her experiences and background. Compare your list to those of your classmates to ensure that you are not planning to survey the same people.

	Participant 1	Participant 2	Participant 3	Participant 4	Participant 5
Name					
Age					
Education					
Background					
Predicted Knowledge					

3. EVALUATION

After you have administered your survey, evaluate the responses you received. Note questions that most people answered correctly, those that most people answered incorrectly, and any unusual or unexpected responses. Also note the sources for your participants' knowledge of psychology. Record your observations in the table below.

Questions Answered Correctly	Questions Answered Incorrectly	Unusual Responses	Sources of Psychology Knowledge

Based on your evaluation, what conclusions can you draw about people's knowledge of psychology? Use the space provided to note your conclusions about the exercise.

_____

_____

_____

_____

4. DISCUSSION

Discuss your conclusions with a small group of classmates. How were your results similar? How were they different? As a group, answer the discussion questions in your textbook. Then use the space below to write a paragraph to explain how people can increase their knowledge and understanding of psychology.

_____

_____

_____

_____

Psychological Methods

Guided Reading

Section 1

READING THE SECTION

DIRECTIONS Read each sentence and fill in the blank with the correct word or phrase.

1. Elements of behavior that exist but cannot be measured directly, such as aggressiveness, are called _____. **(constructs/theories)**

2. For the findings of a scientific study to be confirmed, the study must be _____, or repeated. **(proved/replicated)**

3. A _____ is an educated guess. **(behavior/hypothesis)**

4. Research and experimentation can lead to the _____ of a psychological theory and to the acceptance of its soundness. **(rejection/validation)**

DIRECTIONS On the line provided before each statement, write **T** if a statement is true and **F** if a statement is false. If the statement is false, write the correct term on the line after each sentence that makes the sentence a true statement.

_____ 5. Psychologists begin their studies by framing <u>research questions</u>.

_____

_____ 6. After forming a research question, a psychologist will form a <u>theory</u>, or educated guess.

_____

_____ 7. Psychologists test <u>hypotheses</u> through a variety of methods.

_____

_____ 8. Psychologists might spend many years <u>analyzing</u> the results of their testing.

_____

_____ 9. If a researcher's research observations <u>oppose</u> his or her original theory, then he or she can conclude that the theory is correct.

_____

POST-READING QUICK CHECK

DIRECTIONS In the space provided, write the vocabulary term that best
matches each description.

_____ 10. the act of establishing the soundness of an idea or theory

_____ 11. aspects of behavior that cannot be seen or measured
directly

_____ 12. repeated

_____ 13. educated guess

DIRECTIONS Use vocabulary terms to write a summary of each step
involved in scientific research.

_____

_____

_____

_____

_____

Psychological Methods

READING THE SECTION

DIRECTIONS Read the definitions below. In the space provided, write the letter of the term that matches each definition.

_____ 1. the group a researcher wants to study or describe

_____ 2. a part of a target population

_____ 3. a form containing a set of questions addressed to a statistically significant number of subjects

_____ 4. a predisposition to a certain point of view despite what facts may suggest

a. bias

b. sample

c. questionnaire

d. target population

DIRECTIONS On the line provided before each statement, write **T** if a statement is true and **F** if a statement is false. If the statement is false, write the correct term on the line after each sentence that makes the sentence a true statement.

_____ 5. A <u>random sample</u> of a population always represents the exact proportional makeup of that population.

_____

_____ 6. Questionnaires and <u>interviews</u> are two methods researchers use to conduct surveys and gather information.

_____

_____ 7. The people who volunteer to participate in a survey may reflect a <u>volunteer bias</u>.

_____

_____ 8. A <u>stratified sample</u> of a population is chosen by chance from the general population.

_____

_____ 9. When conducting a survey, it is important to identify your <u>target population</u>.

_____

POST-READING QUICK CHECK

DIRECTIONS In your own words, write the definition of each term.

10. survey: _____

_____

11. target population: _____

_____

12. bias: _____

_____

13. volunteer bias: _____

_____

DIRECTIONS Answer the questions on the lines provided.

14. How are random samples and stratified samples of populations different?

_____

_____

_____

15. How can bias affect the outcome of a survey?

_____

_____

_____

Psychological Methods

READING THE SECTION

DIRECTIONS In the space provided, write the term that best matches each description.

_____ 1. a measure of how closely one thing is related to another

_____ 2. tests that measure people's character traits and temperament

_____ 3. an inherent ability

_____ 4. an in-depth investigation of an individual or group

DIRECTIONS Read each sentence and fill in the blank with the correct word or phrase.

5. _____ observation takes place in a specific area set aside for observation and research. **(Laboratory/Naturalistic)**

6. A relationship in which two factors rise together is known as a

_____ correlation. **(negative/positive)**

7. In the _____ method of research, researchers select a group of participants and then observe them over a period of time. **(cross-sectional/ longitudinal)**

8. A _____ correlation between two factors means that as one factor increases, the other decreases. **(negative/positive)**

9. The _____ method of research involves observing a sample of individuals of different ages. **(cross-sectional/longitudinal)**

10. _____ observation involves observing people in their normal lives, such as at home or at school. **(Laboratory/Naturalistic)**

POST-READING QUICK CHECK
DIRECTIONS Write three words or phrases to describe each term given.

11. case study _____

12. naturalistic observation _____

13. longitudinal method _____

14. correlation _____

15. aptitude _____

DIRECTIONS Use vocabulary terms to write a summary of what you
learned in the section.

_____

_____

_____

_____

_____

Psychological Methods

Guided Reading

Section 4

READING THE SECTION
DIRECTIONS Read each sentence and fill in the blank with the correct
word or phrase.

1. A _____ is an element of an experiment that can change.
   (placebo/variable)

2. A _____ is a substance or treatment that has no effect apart
   from a person's belief in it. **(placebo/preconception)**

3. Members of the _____ group of an experiment do not receive
   treatment. **(control/experimental)**

4. _____ are standards for proper and responsible behavior.
   (Ethics/Variables)

5. In a _____ study, only the experimenters know who is
   receiving treatment. **(single-blind/double-blind)**

DIRECTIONS On the line provided before each statement, write **T** if a
statement is true and **F** if a statement is false. If the statement is false, write
the correct term on the line after each sentence that makes the sentence a
true statement.

_____ 6. The factor that researchers manipulate in an experiment is called the
   <u>dependent</u> variable.

   _____

_____ 7. One way to prevent bias is to conduct a <u>double-blind</u> study, in which neither
   the experimenters nor the participants know who is receiving treatment.

   _____

_____ 8. <u>Standard deviation</u> is a measure of the distance of every score in a test to the
   mean score.

   _____

_____ 9. Confidentiality and avoiding deception are part of the psychologist's code of
   <u>variables</u>.

   _____

POST-READING QUICK CHECK

DIRECTIONS Read the definitions below. In the space provided, write the letter of the name that matches each definition.

_____ 10. a factor in an experiment that can change

_____ 11. a substance or treatment that has no effect apart from a person's belief in it

_____ 12. study in which neither the researchers nor the participants know who receives treatment

_____ 13. opinions formed in advance of adequate knowledge or experience

_____ 14. standards for proper and responsible behavior

a. double-blind study

b. preconceptions

c. ethics

d. variable

e. placebo

DIRECTIONS Answer the questions on the lines provided.

15. How do independent and dependent variables differ in an experiment?

_____

_____

_____

16. Why is it important that psychologists follow a code of ethics?

_____

_____

_____

Psychological Methods   Applying What You've Learned

Experiment

The Hypothetical Snack Bar

Among students at our school, are preferences for cola soft drinks and tortilla chips consistent with preferences when these items are taste-tested?

1. INTRODUCTION
First, read through the experiment in your textbook. Then use this worksheet to help you complete the experiment in your textbook.

2. EXPERIMENT OVERVIEW
When conducting any experiment, you should be careful to follow the steps of the scientific method. Before you begin, you must frame your research question and your initial hypothesis. You should also outline the steps of the experiment and predict what your results will be. Before beginning your taste-testing, complete the graphic organizer below with an overview of the experiment.

Research Question

↓

Hypothesis

↓

Experiment

↓

Predicted Results

3. EXPERIMENT RESULTS

You will be a tester for either the cola or the tortilla chips experiment. As subjects take part in the taste-testing, record their preferences in the chart below. (The column for Option 3 will not be used during the cola test.) When all subjects have completed the test, record the total number of people who preferred each option.

Subject	Preference		
	Option 1	Option 2	Option 3
Total			

4. DISCUSSION

When you have completed your experiment, review the graphic organizer on the previous page. Compare your predicted results to the actual results of the experiment. Hold a group discussion about the experiment and its results, using the discussion questions in your textbook as key points.

After the discussion, use the space below to write a short paragraph to examine how experiments like this one could be important tools for psychologists and other researchers.

_____

_____

_____

_____

Biology and Behavior

READING THE SECTION

DIRECTIONS Read the definitions below. In the space provided, write the letter of the name that matches each definition.

_____ 1. the junction between the axon terminals of one neuron and the dendrites of another

_____ 2. nerve cells

_____ 3. column of nerves that extends from the brain down the back and transmits messages to the muscles and glands in the body

_____ 4. a white fatty substance that insulates and protects axons and speeds the transmission of messages sent by neurons

_____ 5. thin fibers that receive information and pass messages through cell bodies

a. spinal cord

b. synapse

c. dendrites

d. neurons

e. myelin

DIRECTIONS On the line provided before each statement, write **T** if a statement is true and **F** if a statement is false. If the statement is false, write the correct term on the line after each sentence that makes the sentence a true statement.

_____ 6. The brain and spinal cord make up the <u>peripheral</u> nervous system.

_____

_____ 7. The <u>somatic</u> nervous system regulates vital functions like breathing.

_____

_____ 8. Neurons release <u>neurotransmitters</u> to send messages across synapses.

_____

_____ 9. Sensory messages are transmitted by the <u>autonomic</u> nervous system.

_____

_____ 10. The <u>dendrite</u> produces energy that fuels a neuron's activity.

_____

POST-READING QUICK CHECK

DIRECTIONS Read each of the following descriptions, and write who or what is "speaking" in the space provided.

_____ 11. "I am the system that transmits messages from the central nervous system to the rest of the body."

_____ 12. "I am the part of a neuron that transmits messages away from the cell body."

_____ 13. "I am the junction between two neurons."

_____ 14. "I am the part of the central nervous system that runs down the back."

_____ 15. "I am released by neurons to carry messages across synapses."

DIRECTIONS In your own words, write the definition of each term.

16. neuron: _____

_____

17. central nervous system: _____

_____

18. peripheral: _____

_____

Biology and Behavior

Guided Reading
Section 2

READING THE SECTION
DIRECTIONS In the space provided, write the vocabulary term that best matches each description.

_____ 1. part of the brain that regulates balance and coordination

_____ 2. area of the brain that forms a border around the brain stem and is involved in learning, memory, hunger, and aggression

_____ 3. tiny part of the brain that regulates body temperature, nutrient storage, and various aspects of motivation and emotion

_____ 4. largest part of the brain that makes complex learning and abstract thinking possible

_____ 5. part of the brain that regulates heart rate, blood pressure, breathing, and other vital functions

DIRECTIONS Read each sentence and fill in the blank with the correct word or phrase.

6. The brain's _____ areas shape information into meaningful information. **(association/hemispheric)**

7. The outer layer of the brain is known as the cerebral _____. **(callosum/cortex)**

8. The _____ transmits sensory information to the areas of the brain that interpret and respond to the information. **(pons/thalamus)**

9. The midbrain includes the _____ activating system, which regulates alertness and arousal. **(limbic/reticular)**

10. The _____ connects the two hemispheres of the brain. **(cerebrum/corpus callosum)**

POST-READING QUICK CHECK

DIRECTIONS Look at each set of four terms. On the line provided, write the letter of the term that does not relate to the others.

_____ 11. a. cerebrum
        b. complex learning
        c. balance
        d. abstract thinking

_____ 13. a. medulla
        b. forebrain
        c. pons
        d. hypothalamus

_____ 12. a. hemispheres
        b. cerebral cortex
        c. thalamus
        d. motor behavior

_____ 14. a. electroencephalogram
        b. computerized axial
          tomography
        c. limbic system
        d. magnetic resonance imaging

DIRECTIONS Answer the questions on the lines provided.

15. In general, what types of functions do the hindbrain and the midbrain govern?

_____

_____

_____

16. Why do researchers want to learn more about the brain and how it functions?

_____

_____

_____

Biology and Behavior Guided Reading

Section 3

READING THE SECTION

DIRECTIONS Read each sentence and fill in the blank with the correct word or phrase.

1. The _____ system is made up of a series of glands located throughout the body. **(anabolic/endocrine)**

2. _____ are substances that stimulate growth and many kinds of reactions, such as changes in activity levels and physical moods. **(Glands/Hormones)**

3. The _____ gland, sometimes called the "master gland," secretes hormones that affect various aspects of behavior. **(ovary/pituitary)**

4. _____ is the primary male sex hormone. **(Estrogen/Testosterone)**

5. The _____ gland produces a hormone that affects the body's metabolism. **(adrenal/thyroid)**

DIRECTIONS Write three words or phrases to describe each term given.

6. estrogen _____

7. adrenal glands _____

8. testes _____

9. anabolic _____

10. progesterone _____

POST-READING QUICK CHECK
DIRECTIONS Read each of the following descriptions, and write who or
what is "speaking" in the space provided.

_____ 11. "I am the system of glands throughout the body that
produces and releases hormones."

_____ 12. "We are the glands in women that produce estrogen and
progesterone."

_____ 13. "I release a variety of hormones that affect aspects of
behavior and stimulate other glands."

_____ 14. "I help promote increased muscle mass and beard growth
in males."

_____ 15. "I produce thyroxin, which helps control the body's
metabolism."

DIRECTIONS Use vocabulary terms to write a summary of what you
learned in the section.

_____

_____

_____

_____

_____

READING THE SECTION

DIRECTIONS Read the definitions below. In the space provided, write the letter of the name that matches each definition.

_____ 1. the basic building blocks of heredity

_____ 2. threadlike structures that carry genes

_____ 3. an alteration or change in the phase of metabolism in which substances are synthesized into living tissue

_____ 4. the transmission of characteristics from parents to offspring

a. heredity

b. chromosomes

c. mutation

d. genes

DIRECTIONS On the line provided before each statement, write **T** if a statement is true and **F** if a statement is false. If the statement is false, write the correct term on the line after each sentence that makes the sentence a true statement.

_____ 5. Supporters of the <u>nature</u> theory of personality development believe that a person's traits are determined mainly by his or her biological makeup.

_____

_____ 6. <u>Fraternal</u> twins have exactly the same genetic makeup.

_____

_____ 7. The presence of extra <u>chromosomes</u> can lead to physical and behavioral disorders.

_____

_____ 8. The <u>nature</u> theory of personality development says that a person's environment is most important in shaping his or her behavior.

_____

_____ 9. Some genetic disorders are caused by the <u>mutation</u> of genes.

_____

POST-READING QUICK CHECK

DIRECTIONS Read each sentence and fill in the blank with the correct word or phrase.

10. A person's traits are determined by pairs of _____, one inherited from each parent. **(genes/mutations)**

11. To study the roles of heredity and environment in personality development, some

    psychologists study _____ because they share all of the same

    genes. **(first cousins/identical twins)**

12. The _____ issue is related to the roles of biology and environment in the development of personalities. **(adoptee-parent/nature-nurture)**

13. Human genes are found in _____, which are composed of DNA. **(chromosomes/traits)**

14. Genetic disorders can be inherited, or they can be caused by the

    _____ of a gene. **(heredity/mutation)**

DIRECTIONS Answer the questions on the lines provided.

15. What question lies behind the nature-nurture issue?

    _____

    _____

    _____

16. Why do psychologists interested in personality development sometimes study children who have been adopted?

    _____

    _____

    _____

Biology and Behavior   Applying What You've Learned
                                                          Lab

Building the Human Brain

What are the major parts of the brain, and how do they work?

1. INTRODUCTION

First, read through the lab in your textbook. Then use this worksheet to help you complete the lab in your textbook.

2. IDENTIFICATION

Fill out the chart below with a brief description of the function of each part of the brain. You may wish to conduct additional research in the library or on the Internet to learn more about each listed part. Then work with your partner to identify possible images you could use on your mobile to represent each part of the brain. Remember that your chosen images should logically connect to the function of the corresponding part of the brain.

Part	Function	Image
Frontal lobe		
Parietal lobe		
Occipital lobe		
Temporal lobe		
Sensory cortex		
Motor cortex		
Broca's area		
Wernicke's area		
Pons		
Medulla		
Reticular formation		
Cerebellum		
Thalamus		
Hypothalamus		

3. THE FINAL CHALLENGE

After completing your mobile, answer the Final Challenge: Mind Over
Matter questions listed in the textbook. Record your answer to each
question on the appropriate blank below.

1. _____

2. _____

3. _____

4. _____

5. _____

6. _____

7. _____

8. _____

9. _____

10. _____

4. DISCUSSION

With your partner, read and review the discussion questions in your
textbook. In the space below, list key points that the two of you can make
during the class discussion about the lab.

_____

_____

_____

_____

After the class discussion, use the space below to write a short paragraph to
explain how the lab has—or has not—improved your understanding of the
parts and functions of the brain. If you did not find the lab effective, make
suggestions about how it could be improved.

_____

_____

_____

_____

Sensation and Perception   **Guided Reading**

Section 1

READING THE SECTION

DIRECTIONS Read the definitions below. In the space provided, write
the letter of the term that matches each definition.

_____ 1. the weakest amount of a stimulus that can be
sensed

_____ 2. the stimulation of sensory receptors and the
transmission of sensory information

_____ 3. the psychological process through which we
interpret sensory stimulation

_____ 4. the process by which people become more
sensitive to weak stimuli and less sensitive to
unchanging stimuli

_____ 5. the minimum amount of difference that can
be detected between two stimuli

a. difference threshold

b. perception

c. sensory adaptation

d. absolute threshold

e. sensation

DIRECTIONS On the line provided before each statement, write **T** if a
statement is true and **F** if a statement is false. If the statement is false, write
the correct term on the line after each sentence that makes the sentence a
true statement.

_____ 6. Signal-variation theory is a method of distinguishing sensory stimuli that
takes into account a stimulus's strength plus variable elements.

_____

_____ 7. You would not be able to hear a sound that was below your absolute
threshold for hearing.

_____

_____ 8. People who live in cities gradually become less bothered by traffic noise
because of the process called sensory perception.

_____

_____ 9. Something that is variable is subject to change.

_____

POST-READING QUICK CHECK
DIRECTIONS In your own words, write the definition of each term.

10. sensation: _____

_____

11. perception: _____

_____

12. difference threshold: _____

_____

13. variable: _____

_____

DIRECTIONS Answer the questions on the lines provided.

14. What effect do stimuli below a person's absolute threshold have on that person's senses?

_____

_____

_____

15. According to signal-detection theory, what are some factors that can affect sensation and perception?

_____

_____

_____

Sensation and Perception

Guided Reading

Section 2

READING THE SECTION

DIRECTIONS Read each sentence and fill in the blank with the correct word or phrase.

1. Visual _____ is a measure of the sharpness of a person's vision. **(acuity/blindness)**

2. An _____ is the visual impression that remains when an image is removed. **(afterimage/postvision)**

3. The _____ is an opening in the eye through which light enters. **(pupil/retina)**

4. Neurons in the eye that are sensitive to light are called _____. **(lenses/photoreceptors)**

5. _____ colors are located across from each other on the color circle. **(Acute/Complementary)**

DIRECTIONS Read each of the following descriptions, and write who or what is "speaking" in the space provided.

_____ 6. "I am an area in the eye that lacks photoreceptors."

_____ 7. "I am the part of the eye that acts like film in a camera."

_____ 8. "I am the inability to distinguish colors from each other."

_____ 9. "I am a region in the back of the brain that processes visual information."

_____ 10. "I focus vision by changing thickness, based on the distance of an object being viewed."

POST-READING QUICK CHECK

DIRECTIONS Look at each set of four terms. On the line provided, write the letter of the term that does not relate to the others.

_____ 11. a. lens
             b. retina
             c. afterimage
             d. pupil

_____ 13. a. visual acuity
             b. clarity
             c. farsightedness
             d. complementary

_____ 12. a. rod
             b. pupil
             c. photoreceptor
             d. cone

_____ 14. a. color circle
             b. form gray
             c. blind spot
             d. complementary colors

DIRECTIONS Use vocabulary terms to write a summary of what you learned in the section.

_____

_____

_____

_____

_____

Sensation and Perception   Guided Reading

Section 3

READING THE SECTION

DIRECTIONS In the space provided, write the vocabulary term that best matches each description.

_____ 1. a thin layer of tissue that covers or lines an organ

_____ 2. the nerve that transmits neural impulses from the inner ear to the brain

_____ 3. deafness caused by damage to the inner ear, which damages or destroys neurons

_____ 4. a bony tube in the ear that contains the fluids and neurons needed to transmit sounds to the brain

_____ 5. deafness caused by damage to the middle ear, which prevents the amplification of sounds

DIRECTIONS Read each sentence and fill in the blank with the correct word or phrase.

6. Hearing aids can help people who have _____ deafness. **(conductive/sensorineural)**

7. The cochlea is part of the _____ ear, which is protected by a layer of tough bone. **(inner/outer)**

8. Disease and prolonged exposure to very loud sounds can lead to nerve damage and

_____ deafness. **(conductive/sensorineural)**

9. _____, the measure of how high or low a sound is, depends on the sound's frequency. **(Loudness/Pitch)**

10. The loudness of a sound is measured in _____. **(decibels/membranes)**

POST-READING QUICK CHECK

DIRECTIONS On the line provided before each statement, write **T** if a statement is true and **F** if a statement is false. If the statement is false, write the correct term on the line after each sentence that makes the sentence a true statement.

_____ 11. The eardrum is a thin <u>membrane</u> that vibrates when sound waves strike it.

_____

_____ 12. People with <u>conductive</u> deafness are often given cochlear implants to stimulate damaged nerves.

_____

_____ 13. The most significant part of the inner ear is the <u>anvil</u>.

_____

_____ 14. The <u>auditory nerve</u> transmits hearing impulses from the ear to the brain.

_____

_____ 15. The frequency of sound waves determines the sound's <u>loudness</u>.

_____

DIRECTIONS Answer the questions on the lines provided.

16. How are sounds transmitted from the source to the brain?

_____

_____

17. What is the main difference between conductive and sensorineural deafness?

_____

_____

Sensation and Perception

Guided Reading

Section 4

READING THE SECTION
DIRECTIONS Read each sentence and fill in the blank with the correct word or phrase.

1. _____ is the sense that allows people to navigate through a crowded room or touch their noses without looking. **(Kinesthesis/Olfaction)**

2. The _____ sense monitors the body's position in relation to gravity and enables people to keep their balance. **(resilient/vestibular)**

3. The olfactory nerve transmits information about _____ to the brain. **(smell/taste)**

4. According to _____ theory, the nervous system can only process a certain amount of information at a time. **(gate/sensory)**

5. The taste system is _____ and can recover quickly from damage. **(resilient/vestibular)**

DIRECTIONS On the line provided before each statement, write **T** if a statement is true and **F** if a statement is false. If the statement is false, write the correct term on the line after each sentence that makes the sentence a true statement.

_____ 6. The sense of touch registers changes in <u>pressure</u>, temperature, and pain.

_____

_____ 7. The <u>vestibular sense</u> could explain why rubbing an injured area sometimes helps relieve pain.

_____

_____ 8. Without <u>kinesthesis</u>, people would have trouble coordinating movements and exerting fine-motor skills.

_____

_____ 9. People sense <u>taste</u> through receptor neurons located on the tongue.

_____

_____ 10. People can tell when they are standing upright because they possess the <u>olfactory</u> sense.

_____

POST-READING QUICK CHECK

DIRECTIONS Read the definitions below. In the space provided, write the letter of the name that matches each definition.

_____ 11. theory that suggests that the nervous system can only process a certain amount of information at a time

_____ 12. marked by the ability to recover quickly

_____ 13. the sense that informs people about the position and motion of their bodies

_____ 14. nerve that carries scent information to the brain

_____ 15. the sense that monitors the body's position in relation to gravity

a. olfactory nerve

b. kinesthesis

c. gate theory

d. resilient

e. vestibular sense

DIRECTIONS Look at each set of four terms. On the line provided, write the letter of the term that does not relate to the others.

_____ 16. a. olfactory nerve
           b. skin senses
           c. smell
           d. nose

_____ 17. a. kinesthesis
           b. navigation
           c. fine-motor skills
           d. taste buds

_____ 18. a. gate theory
           b. vestibular sense
           c. balance
           d. falling

_____ 19. a. skin senses
           b. vestibular
           c. pressure
           d. pain

Sensation and Perception   **Guided Reading**

READING THE SECTION
DIRECTIONS In the space provided, write the vocabulary term that best matches each description.

_____ 1. visual cues that only need one eye to be perceived

_____ 2. the tendency to perceive a complete or whole figure even though gaps exist

_____ 3. visual cues that require both eyes to be perceived

_____ 4. the use of the rapid progression of still images or objects to produce the illusion of movement

_____ 5. a binocular cue for perceiving depth, based on the difference between the two images of an object that the retina receives as the object moves closer

DIRECTIONS Read each sentence and fill in the blank with the correct word or phrase.

6. The law of _____ says that people assume that objects that move together belong together. **(common fate/similarity)**

7. According to the law of _____, people usually prefer to see smooth patterns such as lines and waves, not disrupted ones. **(continuity/proximity)**

8. The perception of objects against a background is called _____ perception. **(common fate/figure-ground)**

9. People often subconsciously group parts of an image together because of the

_____ of the parts to each other. **(closure/proximity)**

10. The law of _____ says that people usually think of similar items as belonging together. **(continuity/similarity)**

POST-READING QUICK CHECK

DIRECTIONS Read the definitions below. In the space provided, write the letter of the term that matches each definition.

_____ 11. idea that people tend to group similar items together

_____ 12. idea that people tend to group objects that are moving together

_____ 13. idea that people prefer to see smooth patterns rather than disrupted ones

_____ 14. tendency to perceive a complete figure even if gaps exist

_____ 15. illusion of movement caused by the rapid progression of images or objects

a. closure

b. stroboscopic motion

c. law of continuity

d. law of similarity

e. law of common fate

DIRECTIONS Write a word or phrase that means the opposite of each term given.

16. proximity _____

17. static _____

18. continuity _____

**Sensation and
Perception**

Applying What You've Learned
Lab

Sensory Thresholds and Perceptual Organization

*What sensory impressions do you perceive—and which ones do you
filter out?*

1. INTRODUCTION

First, read through the lab in your textbook. Then use this worksheet to
help you complete the lab in your textbook.

2. SENSORY OBSERVATIONS

Use the table below to record the sensory data you observe during the lab.
If you are your group's recorder, list sensations in the table as you observe
them. If you are an illustrator, once the lab is completed, list the sensations
you recorded in your illustrations as well as any others you can recall from
the lab. Mark with a star those that you recall but did not illustrate.

Sights	Sounds	Smells	Tastes	Skin Sensations

3. COMPARISON

After you have completed your list of sensations, compare your list with those of your classmates. Record your observations in the Venn diagram below. In the left circle, list those sensations that only you observed. In the right circle, list those sensations that other people noted that you did not. In the area where the circles overlap, list the sensations that both you and other members of your group recorded.

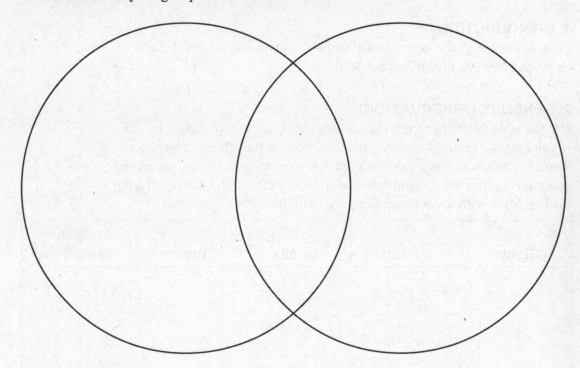

4. DISCUSSION

Read the discussion questions in your textbook, then refer back to the notes you took during your group discussion. With the rest of the class, discuss your results and the conclusions that you can draw from these results.

   After the class discussion, use the space below to write a short paragraph to explain the role the senses play in your daily life. Use at least one sensation you noted during the lab as an example.

_____

_____

_____

_____

Consciousness   Guided Reading

READING THE SECTION

DIRECTIONS In the space provided, write the vocabulary term that best matches each description.

_____ 1. the awareness of things that are both inside and outside ourselves

_____ 2. level at which many basic biological functions occur, such as breathing

_____ 3. focus on a particular stimulus

_____ 4. a concept, model, or schematic idea

_____ 5. state in which a person's sense of self or sense of the world changes

DIRECTIONS Read each sentence and fill in the blank with the correct word or phrase.

6. Like intelligence and emotion, consciousness is considered a psychological

_____ because it cannot be seen or measured.

(construct/selection)

7. The ability to ignore distractions, such as background noise, to pay attention to one

thing is due to _____ attention. **(nonconscious/selective)**

8. _____ ideas are not in your awareness now but can be recalled or remembered. **(Constructed/Preconscious)**

9. According to Sigmund Freud, people have an _____ mind that contains information not available to awareness under most circumstances. **(altered/unconscious)**

10. A person dozing off to sleep experiences an _____ state of consciousness. **(altered/unselected)**

POST-READING QUICK CHECK

DIRECTIONS Look at each set of four terms. On the line provided, write
the letter of the term that does not relate to the others.

_____ 11. a. biological functions   _____ 13. a. preconscious level
      b. breathing   b. unconscious level
      c. nonconscious   c. memories
      d. defense mechanism   d. stored information

_____ 12. a. subconscious   _____ 14. a. sleep
      b. sensory awareness   b. altered state
      c. unconscious   c. changed awareness
      d. hidden   d. wakefulness

DIRECTIONS Answer the questions on the lines provided.

15. What are some of the different ways psychologists use the term *consciousness?*

_____

_____

_____

16. What are four levels of consciousness?

_____

_____

Guided Reading

Section 3

READING THE SECTION

DIRECTIONS Read each of the following descriptions, and write who or what is "speaking" in the space provided.

_____ 1. "I am an altered state of consciousness during which people respond to suggestions and behave as though they are in a trance."

_____ 2. "I am a technique in which a therapist gives instructions during hypnosis that are to be carried out after the session has ended."

_____ 3. "I am something that causes a response."

_____ 4. "I am a method some people use to try to narrow their consciousness and make the stresses of the outside world fade away."

_____ 5. "I am a system that provides information about something happening in the body."

DIRECTIONS Read each sentence and fill in the blank with the correct word or phrase.

6. _____ training enables people to control bodily functions previously regarded as not subject to conscious control. **(Biofeedback/Meditative)**

7. Meditation techniques generally focus on a peaceful, repetitive

_____ to help people relax, such as a light or a chanted

syllable. **(hypnosis/stimulus)**

8. A therapist might use a _____ suggestion to help a person break a habit, such as smoking or overeating. **(biofeedback/posthypnotic)**

9. Some therapists have used _____ to help people recover memories or to prevent pain. **(hypnosis/stimuli)**

10. Meditation, biofeedback, and hypnosis are all possible ways of achieving an

_____ state of consciousness. **(altered/unimpeded)**

POST-READING QUICK CHECK
DIRECTIONS Write three words or phrases to describe each term given.

11. hypnosis _____

12. biofeedback _____

13. meditation _____

14. posthypnotic suggestion _____

DIRECTIONS Answer the questions on the lines provided.

15. Why do some people practice meditation?

_____

_____

_____

16. What are two uses that therapists have found for hypnosis?

_____

_____

Consciousness

READING THE SECTION

DIRECTIONS Read each of the following descriptions, and write who or what is "speaking" in the space provided.

_____ 1. "We are drugs that produce hallucinations."

_____ 2. "We are drugs that increase the activity of the nervous system."

_____ 3. "We are drugs that slow the activity of the nervous system."

_____ 4. "We are stimulants that help people stay awake and reduce appetite."

_____ 5. "We are addictive depressants that have been used to relieve pain and induce sleep."

DIRECTIONS On the line provided before each statement, write **T** if a statement is true and **F** if a statement is false. If the statement is false, write the correct term on the line after each sentence that makes the sentence a true statement.

_____ 6. Intoxication is another word for depression.

_____

_____ 7. Addiction to a drug means that a person's body craves that drug to feel normal.

_____

_____ 8. A hallucination is a perception of an object that seems real but is not.

_____

_____ 9. A euphoria is a false idea that seems real.

_____

_____ 10. Treatment for addiction often includes stimulation, the removal of the harmful substance from the body.

_____

POST-READING QUICK CHECK
DIRECTIONS Read each sentence and fill in the blank with the correct
word or phrase.

11. Some people take _____ to increase their wakefulness or
    alertness or to reduce their appetites. **(depressants/stimulants)**

12. The belief that one can fly is an example of a _____.
    (delusion/detoxification)

13. Drugs that cause people to perceive things that are not really there are called

    _____. **(hallucinogens/narcotics)**

14. _____ can make people feel relaxed but can also have many
    dangerous side effects. **(Depressants/Methamphetamines)**

15. Some drugs can cause feelings of _____, or great happiness,
    among other effects. **(delusion/euphoria)**

DIRECTIONS Look at each set of four terms. On the line provided, write
the letter of the term that does not relate to the others.

_____ 16. a. amphetamines   _____ 18. a. alcohol
         b. stimulants   b. depressants
         c. nicotine   c. amphetamines
         d. alcohol   d. narcotics

_____ 17. a. hallucinogens   _____ 19. a. narcotics
         b. stimulants   b. counseling
         c. marijuana   c. treatment
         d. LSD   d. detoxification

Consciousness

Applying What You've Learned

Experiment

Student Achievement and Sleep Deprivation

What is the connection between adequate sleep and student academic achievement?

1. INTRODUCTION
First, read through the experiment in your textbook. Then use this worksheet to help you complete the experiment in your textbook.

2. EXPERIMENT STEPS
Review the steps necessary to complete the experiment in your textbook. Before you begin the experiment, use the space below to record the details of what you will be doing.

- Hypothesis: _____

  _____

- Population to be studied: _____

  _____

- Sample make-up: _____

  _____

- Control group: _____

  _____

- Experimental group: _____

  _____

- Independent variable(s): _____

- Dependent variable(s): _____

- Variable(s) to remain constant: _____

- Potential confounding variable(s): _____

- Evidence of experimenter bias: _____

- Ethical concerns: _____

  _____

3. OBSERVATIONS

As you conduct your experiment, record your observations in the table below. For each subject you test, record his or her name, whether he or she is part of the control group or experimental group, the variable factors that might affect his or her performance, and the results of your test.

Subject	Group	Variables	Results

After you have completed your experiment, examine the notes you made in the table. What conclusions can you draw about the effects of sleep deprivation on performance? Write a brief analysis in the space below.

_____

_____

_____

4. DISCUSSION

Discuss your conclusions with your classmates and prepare a report to share with the class. Use the space below to record the main points that you will include in the report.

_____

_____

_____

Learning

READING THE SECTION

DIRECTIONS In the space provided, write the vocabulary term that best matches each description.

_____ 1. the act of responding differently to stimuli that are not similar to each other

_____ 2. a type of learning that involves stimulus-response connections

_____ 3. the act of responding in the same ways to stimuli that seem to be similar

_____ 4. a learned avoidance of a particular food

_____ 5. the loss of a stimulus's ability to bring about a conditioned response

DIRECTIONS Read the definitions below. In the space provided, write the letter of the term that matches each definition.

_____ 6. an automatic response to a stimulus

_____ 7. a simple form of learning in which one stimulus calls forth a response normally generated by a different stimulus

_____ 8. a learned response to a stimulus that was previously neutral

_____ 9. a stimulus that causes a response that is not learned

_____ 10. a stimulus that causes a learned response

a. classical conditioning

b. unconditioned stimulus

c. unconditioned response

d. conditioned stimulus

e. conditioned response

POST-READING QUICK CHECK

DIRECTIONS On the line provided before each statement, write **T** if a statement is true and **F** if a statement is false. If the statement is false, write the correct term on the line after each sentence that makes the sentence a true statement.

_____ 11. <u>Counterconditioning</u> is a conditioning method in which people with fears are exposed to harmless stimuli until fear responses are extinguished.

_____

_____ 12. In <u>spontaneous recovery</u>, organisms display responses to stimuli that had been extinguished earlier.

_____

_____ 13. The use of relaxation techniques to help people overcome fears is part of <u>systematic desensitization</u>.

_____

_____ 14. <u>Generalization</u> involves the pairing of pleasant stimuli with fearful ones in order to counteract the subject's fear.

_____

_____ 15. Pavlov's experiments with dogs are an example of <u>classical conditioning</u>.

_____

DIRECTIONS Write three words or phrases to describe each term given.

16. conditioning _____

17. unconditioned response _____

18. extinction _____

19. generalization _____

20. discrimination _____

Learning

READING THE SECTION

DIRECTIONS Read the definitions below. In the space provided, write the letter of the term that matches each definition.

_____ 1. process by which a stimulus increases the chances that a behavior will occur again

_____ 2. method of teaching complex behaviors in which one first reinforces small steps

_____ 3. the relationship in quantity, amount, or size between two things

_____ 4. stimuli that increase the frequency of a behavior that they follow

_____ 5. method of learning in which each step of a sequence leads to another step until the final action is achieved

a. shaping

b. ratio

c. positive reinforcers

d. chaining

e. reinforcement

DIRECTIONS On the line provided before each statement, write **T** if a statement is true and **F** if a statement is false. If the statement is false, write the correct term on the line after each sentence that makes the sentence a true statement.

_____ 6. Rewarding a mouse every time it presses a particular button is an example of <u>partial</u> reinforcement.

_____

_____ 7. Examples of <u>secondary</u> behavior reinforcers include food and warmth.

_____

_____ 8. The <u>schedule of reinforcement</u> outlines how often a behavior is reinforced.

_____

_____ 9. <u>Negative</u> reinforcers are intended to stop unwanted behavior from occurring.

_____

_____ 10. Reinforcement can include both <u>rewards</u> and punishments.

_____

POST-READING QUICK CHECK

DIRECTIONS Read each sentence and fill in the blank with the correct word or phrase.

11. _____ conditioning is a type of learning in which people and animals learn to behave in certain ways because of the results of what they do. **(Operant/Positive)**

12. Money and social status are considered _____ reinforcers because their values must be learned. **(primary/secondary)**

13. Being allowed to visit a friend because you have completed all of your chores is an example of _____ reinforcement. **(negative/positive)**

14. A process such as riding a bicycle can be learned as a series of steps that build on each other, a process known as _____. **(chaining/shaping)**

15. Rewarding a behavior every fifth time it occurs is an example of _____ reinforcement. **(continuous/partial)**

DIRECTIONS In your own words, write the definition of each term.

16. reward: _____

_____

17. reinforcement: _____

_____

18. ratio: _____

_____

19. punishment: _____

_____

20. primary reinforcer: _____

_____

READING THE SECTION

DIRECTIONS In the space provided, write the vocabulary term that best matches each description.

_____ 1. the acquiring of knowledge by observing and imitating other people

_____ 2. learning that remains hidden until it is needed

_____ 3. system in which people are paid to act correctly by earning rewards, such as points that can be cashed in for treats or privileges

_____ 4. form of observational learning in which people observe behavior and can later reproduce it

_____ 5. experienced indirectly through the experience of another person

DIRECTIONS Read each sentence and fill in the blank with the correct word or phrase.

6. Knowing the layout of your school or neighborhood simply because you walk around it on a daily basis is an example of _____ learning.

   (latent/observational)

7. A child learning how to tie a shoe by watching her parents demonstrate how they tie theirs would be an example of _____ learning.

   (latent/observational)

8. Picking up new behaviors by imitating other people is known as

   _____. **(modeling/modifying)**

9. A new student who learns about classroom behavior by observing other students' behavior is demonstrating _____ reinforcement.

   (latent/vicarious)

POST-READING QUICK CHECK

DIRECTIONS Write three words or phrases to describe each term given.

10. latent learning _____

11. observational learning _____

12. modeling _____

13. token economies _____

14. vicarious _____

DIRECTIONS Use vocabulary terms to write a summary of what you
learned in the section.

_____

_____

_____

_____

_____

Learning

Guided Reading

Section 4

READING THE SECTION

DIRECTIONS Read the definitions below. In the space provided, write
the letter of the term that matches each definition.

_____ 1. approach to active learning that includes six
steps to help students absorb information

_____ 2. an effort to learn a great deal of information
all at once

_____ 3. effort to get a general picture of the material
covered in a section of text before reading it

_____ 4. the process of studying something regularly
so the learning is spread over several days or
weeks

a. preview

b. PQ4R method

c. distributed learning

d. massed learning

DIRECTIONS In the space provided, write the step of the PQ4R method
that is being described.

_____ 5. phrasing questions about the material to be studied,
perhaps by changing headings into questions

_____ 6. thinking about material that has been studied in order to
better understand and remember it

_____ 7. repeatedly studying the same material for better
understanding and memory

_____ 8. attempting to get a general picture of the material to be
studied before studying actually begins

_____ 9. stating information about the studied material aloud to
improve memory

_____ 10. examining the material to be studied to try to answer
questions you have phrased about it

POST-READING QUICK CHECK

DIRECTIONS On the line provided before each statement, write **T** if a
statement is true and **F** if a statement is false. If the statement is false, write
the correct term on the line after each sentence that makes the sentence a
true statement.

_____ 11. The <u>PQ4R method</u> of learning was developed by psychologists to help
students better absorb and retain information.

_____

_____ 12. <u>Reciting</u> information that you have studied can help you remember that
information better.

_____

_____ 13. <u>Distributed</u> learning, also sometimes known as cramming, involves a great
deal of study squeezed into a short amount of time.

_____

_____ 14. <u>Massed</u> learning is usually the most effective method of studying.

_____

DIRECTIONS Use vocabulary terms to write a summary of what you
learned in the section.

_____

_____

_____

_____

_____

Learning   Applying What You've Learned

Reinforcement and Discouragement

How can positive reinforcement and discouragement affect people's behavior and performance?

1. INTRODUCTION

First, read through the experiment in your textbook. Then use this worksheet to help you complete the experiment in your textbook.

2. PREPARATION

Once you have identified the students who will serve as your research group, use the table below to sort them into three groups.

Group A	Group B	Group C
1.	1.	1.
2.	2.	2.
3.	3.	3.
4.	4.	4.
5.	5.	5.
6.	6.	6.
7.	7.	7.
8.	8.	8.
9.	9.	9.
10.	10.	10.

When you have sorted your research group, assign roles to the members of your class. Record those roles in the space below.

• Timers: _____

• Assistants:_____

• Recorders:_____

• Pulsetakers:_____

• Encouragers:_____

• Discouragers: _____

3. EXPERIMENT RESULTS

During each day of your experiment, record the number of sit-ups performed by each member of the test group at your station. (The station's recorder will write down this information as the experiment proceeds. Other members of the station team can copy it down later.) Be sure to note which group is being tested at your station each day. Also note whether your station is the encouraging, discouraging, or control station.

Station:			
Participant Number	Day 1 Group _____	Day 2 Group _____	Day 3 Group _____
1.			
2.			
3.			
4.			
5.			
6.			
7.			
8.			
9.			
10.			

4. DISCUSSION

After the experiment is concluded, share your results with the rest of the class. Compare how the various test groups performed at each station. Based on this experiment, what conclusions—if any—can you draw about the effects of reinforcement and discouragement on performance? Summarize your findings below.

_____

_____

_____

_____

Memory   Guided Reading

Section 1

READING THE SECTION

DIRECTIONS Read each of the following descriptions, and write who or what is "speaking" in the space provided.

_____ 1. "I am the process by which a person recollects prior experiences, information, and skills learned in the past."

_____ 2. "I am the translation of information into a form in which it can be stored."

_____ 3. "I am the maintenance of encoded information over a period of time."

_____ 4. "I am the locating of stored information and the returning of it to conscious thought."

_____ 5. "I am any observable event or occurrence."

DIRECTIONS On the line provided before each statement, write **T** if a statement is true and **F** if a statement is false. If the statement is false, write the correct term on the line after each sentence that makes the sentence a true statement.

_____ 6. State-dependent memories can be triggered through emotions.

_____

_____ 7. Repeating information over and over again to keep from forgetting it is known as elaborative rehearsal.

_____

_____ 8. Implicit memories include practiced skills and learned habits.

_____

_____ 9. Semantic memories recall events that happened in our own lives.

_____

_____ 10. Acoustic memory codes represent information in terms of its meaning.

_____

POST-READING QUICK CHECK

DIRECTIONS Read each sentence and fill in the blank with the correct word or phrase.

11. The knowledge that Washington, D.C., is the capital of the United States is an

    example of _____ memory. **(episodic/semantic)**

12. Psychologists refer to the process of locating stored information and returning it to

    conscious thought as _____. **(retrieval/storage)**

13. Visiting a place from your past can trigger _____ memories.
    (context-dependent/state-dependent)

14. The use of sounds to try to remember a piece of information is an example of a(n)

    _____ memory code. **(acoustic/semantic)**

15. _____ memories recall specific information, either from our
    own experiences or from knowledge we have acquired. **(Explicit/Implicit)**

DIRECTIONS Look at each set of four terms. On the line provided, write
the letter of the term that does not relate to the others.

_____ 16. a. retrieval   _____ 18. a. episodic memory
         b. phenomenon   b. implicit memory
         c. encoding   c. personal experience
         d. storage   d. key events

_____ 17. a. repetition   _____ 19. a. state-dependent
         b. maintenance rehearsal   b. past experiences
         c. elaborative rehearsal   c. emotions
         d. memorization   d. semantic memory

Memory

Guided Reading

Section 2

READING THE SECTION

DIRECTIONS Read the definitions below. In the space provided, write the letter of the term that matches each definition.

_____ 1. a mental register of traces of sound

_____ 2. the type or stage of memory capable of large and relatively permanent storage

_____ 3. the immediate recording of data that enter through our senses

_____ 4. memory that holds information briefly before it is either stored in long-term memory or forgotten

_____ 5. brief memories of mental pictures formed of visual stimuli

a. sensory memory

b. short-term memory

c. long-term memory

d. echoic memory

e. iconic memory

DIRECTIONS In the space provided, write the vocabulary term that best matches each description.

_____ 6. the tendency to recall the first items in a series

_____ 7. the organization of items into familiar or manageable units

_____ 8. the replacing of information in short-term memory with new information

_____ 9. the ability to remember visual stimuli over long periods of time

_____ 10. a mental representation formed of the world by organizing bits of information into knowledge

POST-READING QUICK CHECK

DIRECTIONS On the line provided before each statement, write **T** if a statement is true and **F** if a statement is false. If the statement is false, write the correct term on the line after each sentence that makes the sentence a true statement.

_____ 11. Both maintenance rehearsal and elaborative rehearsal can transfer information into <u>short-term</u> memory.

_____

_____ 12. People often recall items at the end of a list better than those in the middle, a phenomenon known as the <u>recency</u> effect.

_____

_____ 13. The echoes of sounds stored in <u>iconic</u> memory can last a long time.

_____

_____ 14. Reducing information you are trying to remember into small, manageable units is called <u>interference</u>.

_____

_____ 15. Two people's memories of an event can differ based on their individual <u>schemas</u>.

_____

DIRECTIONS Answer the questions on the lines provided.

16. What role does short-term memory play in people's lives?

_____

_____

17. How does iconic memory differ from eidetic imagery?

_____

_____

READING THE SECTION

DIRECTIONS In the space provided, write the vocabulary term that best matches each description.

_____ 1. the reacquisition of knowledge that was once known

_____ 2. the identification of objects or events that have been encountered before

_____ 3. the fading away of a memory over time

_____ 4. moved from an original place or location

_____ 5. the bringing to mind of information that has been encountered in the past

DIRECTIONS Read each sentence and fill in the blank with the correct word or phrase.

6. Methods for improving one's memory are called _____.
   (decays/mnemonics)

7. Losing the ability to store new memories is a symptom of

   _____ amnesia. **(anterograde/infantile)**

8. People suffering from _____ amnesia forget the period leading up to a traumatic event. **(anterograde/retrograde)**

9. The loss of memory of early events is called _____ amnesia.
   (infantile/retrograde)

10. In _____, a person does not immediately recognize an item or object but must search his or her memory for information about it.
    (recall/recognition)

POST-READING QUICK CHECK

DIRECTIONS Read the descriptions below. In the space provided, write the letter of the term that matches each description.

_____ 11. severe memory loss

_____ 12. the gradual loss of memory over time

_____ 13. a method used to improve memory

_____ 14. a memory process in which one identifies objects or events that have previously been encountered

_____ 15. nonimmediate retrieval of learned information

a. mnemonic

b. decay

c. recall

d. amnesia

e. recognition

DIRECTIONS Use vocabulary terms to write a summary of what you learned in the section.

_____

_____

_____

_____

_____

Memory # Applying What You've Learned

Effective Memory Improvement

Which method of memorization is most effective?

1. INTRODUCTION

First, read through the experiment in your textbook. Then use this worksheet to help you complete the experiment in your textbook.

2. BACKGROUND KNOWLEDGE

Have each member of your group select one memorization technique discussed in the textbook chapter. Write your selected technique in the center of the graphic organizer below. In the surrounding ovals, list suggestions for situations in which that technique might be useful. You may wish to add additional ovals to your graphic organizer as necessary.

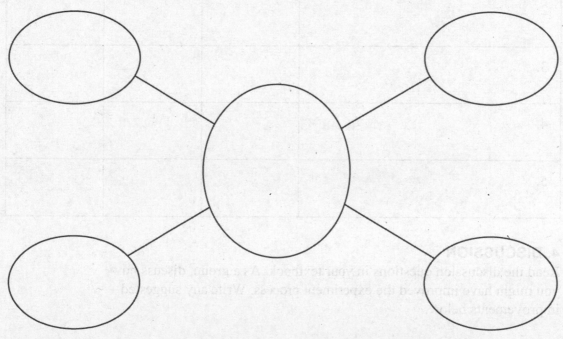

After all group members have completed their organizers, compare your notes. Decide which three memorization techniques you will test in this experiment. Explain why you have chosen them in the space below.

_____

_____

_____

_____

3. EXPERIMENT RESULTS

As you conduct your memory experiment, record the results in the table below. Be sure to note which memorization technique is used for each of the subjects' attempts.

Memorization Methods Used

Try 1: _____

Try 2: _____

Try 3: _____

Subject	Try 1	Try 2	Try 3
1.			
2.			
3.			
4.			
5.			

4. DISCUSSION

Read the discussion questions in your textbook. As a group, discuss how you might have improved the experiment process. Write any suggested improvements below.

_____

_____

_____

_____

Thinking and Language   Guided Reading

READING THE SECTION
DIRECTIONS In the space provided, write the vocabulary term that best matches each description.

_____ 1. an object or act that stands for something else

_____ 2. brought into alignment with other similar tests

_____ 3. a mental structure used to categorize objects, people, or events that share similar characteristics

_____ 4. to show or illustrate by example

_____ 5. the mental activity involved in understanding, processing, and communicating information

DIRECTIONS Read each sentence and fill in the blank with the correct word or phrase.

6. Creative people often excel at _____ thinking, in which a person devises many different solutions to a problem. **(convergent/divergent)**

7. A _____ is a particular example of a concept or item, one that best represents its characteristics. **(prototype/symbol)**

8. _____, or directed, thinking involves looking at a problem and narrowing all possible options to one solution. **(Convergent/Divergent)**

9. Monkeys, chickens, and fish all belong under the _____ of "animal." **(concept/symbol)**

10. Drivers know to stop when they see a red octagonal sign because the sign functions

as a _____. **(prototype/symbol)**

POST-READING QUICK CHECK

DIRECTIONS On the line provided before each statement, write **T** if a statement is true and **F** if a statement is false. If the statement is false, write the correct term on the line after each sentence that makes the sentence a true statement.

_____ 11. Because the questions on most standardized tests have only one correct answer, they measure <u>divergent</u> thinking.

_____

_____ 12. Thinking about how people think is an example of <u>metacognition</u>.

_____

_____ 13. <u>Divergent</u> thinking often leads to creative solutions.

_____

_____ 14. To <u>exemplify</u> an idea is to illustrate its characteristics through examples.

_____

_____ 15. A <u>prototype</u> is a mental group of objects, people, events, or ideas that have similar characteristics.

_____

DIRECTIONS Write three words or phrases to describe each term given.

16. thinking _____

17. metacognition _____

18. symbol _____

19. standardized _____

20. prototype _____

Thinking and Language   Guided Reading

READING THE SECTION

DIRECTIONS Read the definitions below. In the space provided, write
the letter of the term that matches each definition.

_____ 1. situations or scenarios	a. flexibility
_____ 2. a procedure that, when used properly, will lead to the solution of a problem	b. mental set
_____ 3. the mental rearrangement of elements of a problem	c. algorithm
	d. recombination
_____ 4. the ability to overcome rigidity	e. circumstances
_____ 5. the tendency to respond to a new problem with an approach that was successfully used in similar problems	

DIRECTIONS In the space provided, write the vocabulary term that best
matches each description.

_____ 6. a strategy for making judgments and solving problems; rules of thumb

_____ 7. a problem-solving method that involves reducing the difference between the present situation and the desired one

_____ 8. the tendency to arrive at a solution after a period of time away from the problem

_____ 9. a barrier to problem solving that involves the tendency to think of objects only in terms of their common uses

_____ 10. a heuristic device based on the assumption that certain actions will have certain results

POST-READING QUICK CHECK

DIRECTIONS On the line provided before each statement, write **T** if a statement is true and **F** if a statement is false. If the statement is false, write the correct term on the line after each sentence that makes the sentence a true statement.

_____ 11. A mathematical formula that will always yield the right answer to a problem is an example of an <u>algorithm</u>.

_____

_____ 12. The <u>means-end analysis</u> technique of problem solving involves reducing the difference between your current situation and the desired outcome.

_____

_____ 13. Some problems can be solved through <u>analogies</u> that express similarities between two or more items or situations.

_____

_____ 14. A <u>heuristic</u> approach to problem solving is based on rules of thumb and may not work every time.

_____

_____ 15. The inability to view objects as having more than one function is called <u>mental set</u>.

_____

DIRECTIONS Answer the questions on the lines provided.

16. What effect does mental set have on problem solving?

_____

_____

17. How can the incubation effect help people solve problems?

_____

_____

Thinking and Language   **Guided Reading**

READING THE SECTION
DIRECTIONS Read each of the following descriptions, and write who or what is "speaking" in the space provided.

_____ 1. "I am the use of information to reach conclusions."

_____ 2. "I am a listing of various reasons for or against making a particular choice."

_____ 3. "I am an idea or statement that provides the basic information needed to draw conclusions."

_____ 4. "I am a form of reasoning that draws on individual cases or particular facts to reach a general conclusion."

_____ 5. "I am a form of reasoning that draws specific conclusions based on a given set of premises."

DIRECTIONS Read each sentence and fill in the blank with the correct word or phrase.

6. The _____ heuristic allows people to make decisions based on the information available in their immediate consciousnesses. **(availability/representative)**

7. When people make decisions based on their personal ideas or standards, they are

   using the _____ heuristic. **(anchoring/availability)**

8. A decision made about a sample according to the population that the sample seems to

   represent, was made using the _____ heuristic.

   (anchoring/representative)

9. A conclusion made using _____ reasoning will always be true if the premises on which it is based are true. **(deductive/inductive)**

10. Because they are general statements, the conclusions that we make with

   _____ reasoning cannot always be proven true, though many

   can be proven false. **(deductive/inductive)**

POST-READING QUICK CHECK

DIRECTIONS Look at each set of four terms. On the line provided, write
the letter of the term that does not relate to the others.

_____ 11. a. availability heuristic
             b. deductive reasoning
             c. specific conclusions
             d. premises

_____ 13. a. representative
             b. deductive
             c. anchoring
             d. availability

_____ 12. a. pluses and minuses
             b. decision making
             c. balance sheet
             d. random chance

_____ 14. a. general conclusion
             b. individual cases
             c. balance sheet
             d. inductive reasoning

DIRECTIONS In your own words, write the definition of each term.

15. premise: _____

_____

16. reasoning: _____

_____

17. deductive reasoning: _____

_____

18. inductive reasoning: _____

_____

19. availability heuristic: _____

_____

20. representative heuristic: _____

_____

Thinking and Language   Guided Reading

READING THE SECTION

DIRECTIONS Read the definitions below. In the space provided, write the letter of the name that matches each definition.

_____ 1. the communication of ideas through symbols that are arranged according to rules of grammar

_____ 2. units of meaning in a language

_____ 3. the way in which words are arranged to make phrases and sentences

_____ 4. the study of meaning

_____ 5. the basic sounds of a language

a. morphemes

b. language

c. semantics

d. phonemes

e. syntax

DIRECTIONS On the line provided before each statement, write **T** if a statement is true and **F** if a statement is false. If the statement is false, write the correct term on the line after each sentence that makes the sentence a true statement.

_____ 6. The psychology of language is called <u>semantics</u>.

_____

_____ 7. <u>Overregulation</u> is a common error among children learning to speak a language.

_____

_____ 8. The <u>language acquisition device</u> enables the brain to understand grammar, allowing people to learn languages.

_____

_____ 9. The ability to speak two languages is called <u>bilingualism</u>.

_____

_____ 10. Prefixes and suffixes that can be added to words are examples of <u>phonemes</u>.

_____

POST-READING QUICK CHECK

DIRECTIONS Read each sentence and fill in the blank with the correct word or phrase.

11. The English language uses about 43 distinct _____, or basic sounds. **(phonemes/syntaxes)**

12. The application of normal grammar rules in situations to which they do not apply is

    called _____. **(language acquisition/overregulation)**

13. The relationship between language and the things it depicts is called

    _____. **(phonemes/semantics)**

14. _____ refers to the way in which words are arranged in a phrase or sentence. **(Semantics/Syntax)**

15. Psychologists called the natural tendency of people to learn language a

    _____ device. **(language acquisition/overregulation)**

DIRECTIONS Answer the questions on the lines provided.

16. What are some things people use language for?

    _____

    _____

    _____

17. What are the three basic elements of a language?

    _____

    _____

    _____

Thinking and Language   Applying What You've Learned

Children, Thinking, and Language

Help new parents understand how their child will think, solve problems, and use language in these processes.

1. INTRODUCTION
First, read through the lab in your textbook. Then use this worksheet to help you complete the lab in your textbook.

2. TOPIC ANALYSIS
With the other members of your group, brainstorm important terms, concepts, and ideas about your assigned topic. Use the concept map below to organize your thoughts. First, write your topic in the center rectangle. Then list related terms, concepts, and ideas in the surrounding ovals. You may add additional ovals as necessary.

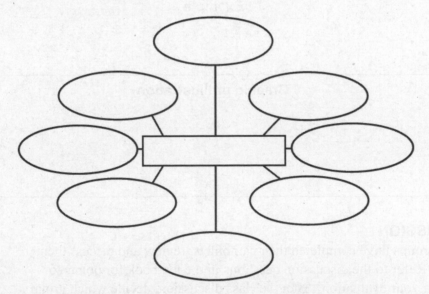

After your group has completed brainstorming, work together to identify the most important points to share with new parents. Consult the list of important information in the textbook under Step 3, Sharing Your Experience. In the space below, list the points you will share.

_____

_____

_____

_____

3. PAMPHLET PLAN

After you have been assigned to a new group, share your key points with your new partners. Then plan your section of the pamphlet that your group will produce. Use the table below to organize the information you will want to include.

Key Information/Main Ideas
•   •   •   •   •
Important Terms
•   •
Example
Graphic or Illustration

4. DISCUSSION

Once all groups have completed their pamphlets, review and discuss them as a class. Refer to the discussion questions in the textbook for points to consider in your evaluation. After the class discussion, decide which group produced what you consider to be the most helpful pamphlet for new parents. In the space below, explain why you think it is helpful.

_____

_____

_____

_____

Intelligence

READING THE SECTION

DIRECTIONS In the space provided, write the vocabulary term that best matches each description.

_____ 1. the abilities to learn from experience, to think rationally, and to deal effectively with others

_____ 2. knowledge and skills gained from experience

_____ 3. ability or aptitude

_____ 4. theory proposed by Robert Sternberg that suggests intelligence can be broken into three distinct factors: analytical, creative, and practical intelligence

DIRECTIONS Read the descriptions below. In the space provided, write the letter of the term that matches each description.

_____ 5. abilities to perform tasks such as negotiating or changing a tire; also called street smarts

_____ 6. according to Daniel Goleman, type of intelligence that consists of five factors that are involved in success

_____ 7. ability to paint, write, cook, and perform other similar activities

_____ 8. the type of intelligence used in academic courses

_____ 9. theory proposed by Howard Gardner that people have different types of intelligence, such as verbal, visual-spatial, and intrapersonal intelligences

a. multiple intelligence

b. practical intelligence

c. analytical intelligence

d. creative intelligence

e. emotional intelligence

DIRECTIONS On the line provided before each statement, write **T** if a statement is true and **F** if a statement is false. If the statement is false, write the correct term on the line after each sentence that makes the sentence a true statement.

_____ 10. <u>Facility</u>, including the ability to learn from experience, is the main characteristic that sets humans apart from other animals.

_____

_____ 11. A test that covers one particular subject can reflect a student's level of <u>achievement</u>.

_____

_____ 12. The theory that people excel in any of several different types of intelligence, including kinesthetic and musical intelligences, is called <u>emotional</u> intelligences.

_____

_____ 13. Self-awareness, mood management, self-motivation, impulse control, and people skills are all aspects of <u>analytical</u> intelligence.

_____

_____ 14. <u>Intelligence</u> varies widely from person to person.

_____

DIRECTIONS Use vocabulary terms to write a summary of what you learned in the section.

_____

_____

_____

_____

_____

Intelligence

READING THE SECTION

DIRECTIONS Read the descriptions below. In the space provided, write the letter of the name that matches each description.

_____ 1. a number that reflects the relationship between a person's mental age and his or her chronological age

_____ 2. the consistency of a test

_____ 3. to judge or determine

_____ 4. the measure of whether a test measures what it is supposed to measure

_____ 5. a measure of the intellectual age at which a person is functioning

a. assess

b. reliability

c. validity

d. intelligence quotient

e. mental age

DIRECTIONS On the line provided before each statement, write **T** if a statement is true and **F** if a statement is false. If the statement is false, write the correct term on the line after each sentence that makes the sentence a true statement.

_____ 6. Psychologists sometimes modify raw test scores into <u>transformed</u> scores to make comparisons easier.

_____

_____ 7. A test can be considered <u>reliable</u> if it gives similar scores each time it is used.

_____

_____ 8. A test can be said to have <u>reliability</u> if it measures what it is intended to measure.

_____

_____ 9. A person's <u>intelligence quotient</u> can be measured through one of two distinct tests.

_____

_____ 10. <u>Test-retest reliability</u> is a measure of the intellectual level at which a person functions.

_____

POST-READING QUICK CHECK

DIRECTIONS Read each of the following descriptions, and write who or what is "speaking" in the space provided.

_____ 11. "I am a measure of the level at which a person functions."

_____ 12. "I am a method of checking the reliability of a test by having one person take it multiple times."

_____ 13. "I am a number that reflects the relationship between a person's mental age and his or her chronological age."

_____ 14. "I am a test score that has been modified in a systematic fashion."

DIRECTIONS In your own words, write the definition of each term.

15. reliability: _____

_____

16. validity: _____

_____

17. assess: _____

_____

Intelligence

READING THE SECTION

DIRECTIONS In the space provided, write the vocabulary term that best matches each description.

_____ 1. the ability to invent new solutions to problems or to create original or ingenious materials

_____ 2. possessing outstanding talent or showing the potential for performing at remarkably high levels of accomplishment when compared to other people of the same age, experience, or environment

_____ 3. reduced or weakened

_____ 4. intellectual functioning that is below average, as indicated by an intelligence score at or below 70

_____ 5. a person who develops special skill in a particular talent or discipline in childhood

DIRECTIONS Read each sentence and fill in the blank with the correct word or phrase.

6. Mental _____ can be classified as mild, moderate, severe, or profound. **(creativity/retardation)**

7. Because he had begun composing music by age 5, Wolfgang Amadeus Mozart can be considered a _____. **(prodigy/savant)**

8. The abilities to paint portraits, compose symphonies, and propose new scientific theories are examples of _____. **(creativity/retardation)**

9. A _____ is a person who has mental retardation or autism but exhibits extraordinary skill in a particular field. **(prodigy/savant)**

10. People who are _____ display high levels of ability when compared to others. **(diminished/gifted)**

POST-READING QUICK CHECK
DIRECTIONS Write three words or phrases to describe each term given.

11. prodigy _____

12. diminished _____

13. mental retardation _____

14. gifted _____

15. creativity _____

DIRECTIONS Use vocabulary terms to write a summary of what you
learned in the section.

_____

_____

_____

_____

_____

Intelligence

READING THE SECTION

DIRECTIONS Read each sentence and fill in the blank with the correct word or phrase.

1. _____ is the extent to which variations in a trait from person to person can be explained by genetic factors. **(Heritability/Intelligence)**

2. The mental capacities that allow people to respond quickly to situations or problems are part of _____ intelligence. **(crystallized/fluid)**

3. _____ intelligence is the sum of a person's knowledge of the world. **(Crystallized/Fluid)**

4. A person's _____ are the people with whom he or she works and associates. **(colleagues/siblings)**

5. _____ programs are designed to provide young children with enriched early experiences. **(Genetic/Preschool)**

DIRECTIONS On the line provided before each statement, write **T** if a statement is true and **F** if a statement is false. If the statement is false, write the correct term on the line after each sentence that makes the sentence a true statement.

_____ 6. As a person ages, his or her <u>crystallized</u> intelligence may change, leading to decreased response times.

_____

_____ 7. Scientists estimate that the <u>heritability</u>, or genetic influence, of intelligence ranges from 40 to 60 percent.

_____

_____ 8. <u>Fluid</u> intelligence, or general knowledge, often continues to grow as people age.

_____

_____ 9. A psychologist working on a study might seek out the thoughts and opinions of his or her <u>colleagues</u>.

_____

POST-READING QUICK CHECK

DIRECTIONS Read the descriptions below. In the space provided, write the letter of the name that matches each description.

_____ 10. co-workers or associates

_____ 11. the sum of a person's knowledge about the
world

_____ 12. the extent to which variations in a trait from
person to person can be explained by genetic
factors

_____ 13. the mental capacities that allow people to
respond quickly to situations or problems

a. heritability

b. colleagues

c. crystallized intelligence

d. fluid intelligence

DIRECTIONS Answer the questions on the lines provided.

14. How can heritability affect a person's intelligence?

_____

_____

_____

15. How can fluid intelligence change over time?

_____

_____

_____

Intelligence   Applying What You've Learned
                                                              Lab

Profile of a Genius

What are the most important qualities for a genius to have? Who has met the profile of a genius?

1. INTRODUCTION
First, read through the lab in your textbook. Then use this worksheet to help you complete the lab in your textbook.

2. PROFILE CREATION
Once your group has determined which theory of intelligence and which method of testing you will focus on, work together to create a genius profile. In the space below, list the basic headings on which you will base your profile. Below each heading, list specific points you would consider genius. For each heading you create, prepare a defense of your choices.

Genius Profile

Heading 1: _____

- _____
- _____
- _____

Defense: _____

Heading 2: _____

- _____
- _____
- _____

Defense: _____

Heading 3: _____

- _____
- _____
- _____

Defense: _____

3. TEST RESULTS

Once each group has compiled its genius profile, work together as a class to test some individuals commonly considered geniuses. For each individual tested, conduct research to learn about his or her achievements. Based on that information, determine which group's profile is most applicable to the subject in question and use that profile to analyze him or her. Use your analysis to conclude whether each subject was a genius or average. Record your conclusions in the table below.

Subject	Achievements	Profile to Be Used	Conclusion

4. DISCUSSION

After all analyses are completed, conduct a class discussion on the subject of genius. What qualifies an individual to be considered a genius? Do the qualifications differ from person to person? Use the space below to write a short paragraph expressing your views of the nature of genius.

_____

_____

_____

_____

Infancy and Childhood

READING THE SECTION
DIRECTIONS In the space provided, write the vocabulary term that best matches each description.

_____ 1. a period or level in the development process that is distinct from other levels

_____ 2. the field in which psychologists study how people grow and change throughout the life span

_____ 3. type of psychological study in which researchers select a particular group of participants and then observe that same group for a period of time

_____ 4. the automatic and sequential process of development that results from genetic signals

_____ 5. a stage or point in development during which a person is best suited to learn a particular skill or behavior pattern

DIRECTIONS Read each sentence and fill in the blank with the correct word or phrase.

6. Research suggests that early childhood may be a _____ period for the development of language skills, as children pick these skills up more easily than adults do. **(critical /longitudinal)**

7. Because _____ is a sequential process, infants generally learn to sit up before they can crawl and to crawl before they can stand. **(continuity/ maturation)**

8. Each _____ in the development process is distinct from every other one. **(blank slate/stage)**

9. Conception, infancy, childhood, adolescence, and adulthood are all topics of interest to _____ psychologists. **(cross-sectional/developmental)**

10. _____ development happens gradually over a long period of time. **(Continuous/Stage)**

POST-READING QUICK CHECK

DIRECTIONS Write three words or phrases to describe each term given.

11. developmental psychology: _____

_____

12. maturation: _____

_____

13. stage: _____

_____

14. critical period: _____

_____

15. continuous development: _____

_____

DIRECTIONS Use vocabulary terms to write a summary of what you learned in the section.

_____

_____

_____

_____

_____

Infancy and Childhood

READING THE SECTION

DIRECTIONS Read the definition below. In the space provided, write the letter of the name that matches each definiton.

_____ 1. the system of organs and passages involved in the intake and exchange of oxygen and carbon dioxide between a living organism and its environment

_____ 2. an involuntary reaction or response

_____ 3. the period of life from two years old to adolescence

_____ 4. the development of purposeful movement

_____ 5. the period of life from birth to two years

a. infancy

b. reflex

c. motor development

d. respiratory system

e. childhood

DIRECTIONS On the line provided before each statement, write **T** if a statement is true and **F** if a statement is false. If the statement is false, write the correct term on the line after each sentence that makes the sentence a true statement.

_____ 6. During <u>childhood</u>, which begins right after birth, dramatic gains in height and weight occur.

_____

_____ 7. Swallowing, which happens involuntarily, is an example of a <u>reflex</u>.

_____

_____ 8. <u>Perceptual</u> development gradually leads to the replacement of reflex actions with more purposeful movements.

_____

_____ 9. Changes in how infants react to different stimuli are the result of <u>motor</u> development.

_____

_____ 10. The <u>respiratory</u> system is necessary to sustain life.

_____

POST-READING QUICK CHECK

DIRECTIONS Read each of the following descriptions, and write who or
what is "speaking" in the space provided.

_____ 11. "I am the period of life that begins with birth and lasts
about two years."

_____ 12. "I am the period of life that begins at age two and
continues until adolescence."

_____ 13. "I am the system of the body that takes in and exchanges
oxygen and carbon dioxide."

_____ 14. "I am an involuntary reaction or response."

_____ 15. "I am the process by which infants learn to make sense
of sights, sounds, tastes, and other sensations."

DIRECTIONS Write a word or phrase that means the opposite of each
term given.

16. infancy _____

17. reflex _____

18. motor development _____

Infancy and Childhood

READING THE SECTION

DIRECTIONS Read the descriptions below. In the space provided, write the letter of the name that matches each description.

_____ 1. parenting style that combines warmth with age-appropriate rules and responsibilities

_____ 2. the process by which some animals form immediate attachments during a critical period

_____ 3. the emotional ties that form between people

_____ 4. parenting style that emphasizes obedience for its own sake

_____ 5. the value or worth that people attach to themselves

a. attachment

b. authoritarian

c. authoritative

d. self-esteem

e. imprinting

DIRECTIONS In the space provided, write the vocabulary term that best matches each description.

_____ 6. the instinctual need to touch and be touched by something soft

_____ 7. the expression of love or esteem given only when an individual exhibits suitable behavior

_____ 8. distress that occurs when an infant is left by his or her mother

_____ 9. fear of strangers

_____ 10. a consistent expression of love and acceptance shown regardless of changing situations or behaviors

POST-READING QUICK CHECK

DIRECTIONS Read each sentence and fill in the blank with the correct
word or phrase.

11. Feelings of _____ keep people, such as children and their
    parents, together. **(attachment/imprinting)**

12. Some psychologists believe that children want _____ and feel
    the need to be touched by something soft, such as skin or fur . **(contact comfort/
    self-esteem)**

13. Children who receive _____ positive rewards may feel
    worthwhile only when they are doing what their parents or authority figures want
    them to do. **(conditional/unconditional)**

14. _____, the value that people attach to themselves, helps protect
    people against the stresses and struggles of life. **(Positive regard/Self-esteem)**

15. Parents who are _____ stress obedience over everything else.
    (authoritarian/authoritative)

DIRECTIONS In your own words, write the definition of each term.

16. unconditional positive regard: _____

    _____

17. separation anxiety: _____

    _____

18. authoritative: _____

    _____

19. stranger anxiety: _____

    _____

20. imprinting: _____

    _____

Infancy and Childhood

Guided Reading

Section 4

READING THE SECTION

DIRECTIONS In the space provided, write the vocabulary term that best matches each description.

_____ 1. according to Kohlberg, a level of moral development in which moral judgments are based on fear of punishment or desire for pleasure

_____ 2. the inability to see another person's point of view

_____ 3. not part of concrete existence; theoretical

_____ 4. the understanding that objects exist even when they cannot be seen or touched

_____ 5. according to Piaget, the stage of cognitive development during which people begin to think logically about abstract concepts

DIRECTIONS Read each sentence and fill in the blank with the correct word or phrase.

6. In Piaget's _____ stage of development, infants begin to understand that there is a relationship between their physical movements and the results they sense. **(preoperational/sensorimotor)**

7. The _____ stage is when most children begin to show signs of adult thinking, though they do not yet think logically about abstract concepts. **(concrete-operational/formal-operational)**

8. During the _____ stage of development, children use words and language but think in only one dimension. **(concrete-operational/ preoperational)**

9. _____ moral reasoning is based on the consequences of behavior. **(Conventional/Preconventional)**

10. Reasoning based on a person's own moral standards of goodness is called

_____ moral reasoning. **(postconventional/preconventional)**

POST-READING QUICK CHECK

DIRECTIONS Read the descriptions below. In the space provided, write the letter of the term that matches each description.

_____ 11. the stage of cognitive development during which children acquire the ability to think logically

_____ 12. the level of moral development at which a person makes judgments based on conventional standards of right and wrong

_____ 13. the level of moral development during which moral judgments are derived from a person's own moral standards

_____ 14. the stage during which a child learns to use language but does not yet think logically

_____ 15. the level of moral development in which moral judgments are based on fear of punishment or desire for pleasure

a. conventional moral reasoning

b. postconventional moral reasoning

c. preconventional moral reasoning

d. concrete-operational stage

e. preoperational stage

DIRECTIONS Answer the questions on the lines provided.

16. Why would your life be different if you did not have a sense of object permanence?

_____

_____

_____

17. What do psychologists mean by egocentrism?

_____

_____

_____

Infancy and Childhood   Applying What You've Learned
                                                              Lab

Prenatal and Postnatal Development

How do fetuses and infants develop in the United States and in other parts of the world?

1. INTRODUCTION

First, read through the lab in your textbook. Then use this worksheet to help you complete the lab in your textbook.

2. DEVELOPMENT RESEARCH

Once your teacher has organized the class into groups A and B, work with the members of your group to assign teams to research particular topics. When you begin your research, use the table below to organize your notes. In the left column, list topics to be researched. For example, if you are part of Group A researching prenatal development, your topics might include Organs and Systems, Activities, and so on. After you have listed your topics, use the column on the right to record your findings about each.

Group: _____

Topic to be studied: _____

Topic	Findings

3. INTERNATIONAL COMPARISON

For the second part of your lab, you will research a prenatal or cultural practice that might lead to developmental differences between children in another country and children in the United States. Use the concept map below to record your findings. In the top oval, identify the country on which you have focused your research. In the next oval, list the practice that you are studying. Use the remaining ovals to list ways in which that practice can affect the prenatal or postnatal development of children. You may wish to add more ovals to accommodate more information.

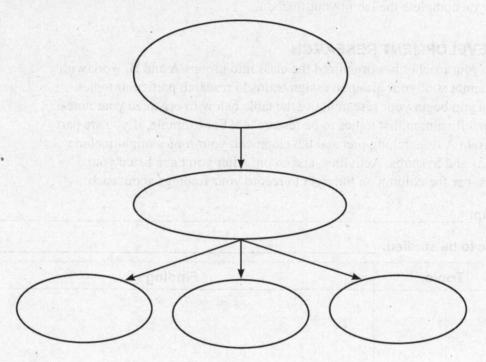

4. DISCUSSION

Once all teams have presented their findings to the class, have a class discussion using the questions in the textbook as a guide. In the space below, describe what you found most surprising about the results of this lab. Why were you surprised by this information?

_____

_____

_____

_____

Adolescence

Guided Reading

Section 1

READING THE SECTION

DIRECTIONS Read the definitions below. In the space provided, write
the letter of the term that matches each definition.

_____ 1. the organs that make sexual reproduction
possible, such as the ovaries and testes

_____ 2. a sudden burst of physical growth during
which adolescents gain height and weight

_____ 3. a female's first menstrual period

_____ 4. the onset of one's ability to reproduce

_____ 5. sexual characteristics not involved in
reproduction

a. adolescent growth spurt

b. puberty

c. primary sex
characteristics

d. secondary sex
characteristics

e. menarche

DIRECTIONS On the line provided before each statement, write **T** if a
statement is true and **F** if a statement is false. If the statement is false, write
the correct term on the line after each sentence that makes the sentence a
true statement.

_____ 6. Examples of <u>primary sex characteristics</u> are facial hair in males and rounded
hips and breasts in females.

_____

_____ 7. <u>Secondary sex characteristics</u> include the ovaries and testes.

_____

_____ 8. The <u>adolescent growth spurt</u> usually lasts two to three years.

_____

_____ 9. The <u>menarche</u> is a major life event for most girls.

_____

_____ 10. Adolescence begins with the onset of <u>puberty</u> and ends when physical growth
does.

_____

POST-READING QUICK CHECK

DIRECTIONS Read each sentence and fill in the blank with the correct word or phrase.

11. The _____ usually lasts two to three years.
    (adolescent growth spurt/menarche)

12. Adolescence begins with the onset of _____, the changes that lead to the ability to reproduce. **(primary sex characteristics/puberty)**

13. The deepening of the voice in males is an example of a _____. **(primary sex characteristic/secondary sex characteristic)**

14. The first menstruation, or _____, usually occurs in girls between the ages of 11 and 14. **(menarche/puberty)**

15. The period of sudden adolescent growth is sometimes called the

    _____ because parts of their body grow at different rates.

    (awkward age/menarche)

DIRECTIONS In your own words, write the definition of each term.

16. puberty: _____

    _____

17. menarche: _____

    _____

18. primary sex characteristics: _____

    _____

19. secondary sex characteristics: _____

    _____

Adolescence

Guided Reading
Section 2

READING THE SECTION
DIRECTIONS Read each of the following descriptions, and write who or what is "speaking" in the space provided.

_____ 1. "I am a peer group of 5 to 10 people who spend a great deal of time with one another, sharing activities and confidences."

_____ 2. "I am a large group of people who do not necessarily spend a lot of time together, but share attitudes and group identity."

_____ 3. "I am active in groups where I try to get each individual to conform to the goals, attitudes, and behaviors of the group."

_____ 4. " I am a biological factor that has some effect on the activity levels, moods swings, and aggressive tendencies of adolescence."

_____ 5. "I am the relationship that adolescents struggle with as they develop closer relationships with peers."

DIRECTIONS Read the definitions below. In the space provided, write the letter of the term that matches each definition.

_____ 6. during adolescence these relationships undergo redefinition

_____ 7. peer groups who spend a great deal of time with one another

_____ 8. pressure from friends to conform to their goals, attitudes, and behavior

_____ 9. large groups of people who share attitudes and group identity

_____ 10. translates as "storm and stress"

a. cliques

b. crowds

c. peer pressure

d. relationships with parents

e. sturm und drang

POST-READING QUICK CHECK

DIRECTIONS On the line provided before each statement, write **T** if a statement is true and **F** if a statement is false. If the statement is false, write the correct term on the line after each sentence that makes the sentence a true statement.

_____ 11. Adolescence is a time of <u>sturm und drang</u>.

_____

_____ 12. A <u>crowd</u> is a group of people who spend a great deal of time together.

_____

_____ 13. <u>Peer pressure</u> is relatively weak in early adolescence but increases in middle adolescence.

_____

_____ 14. Adolescents are involved in a quest for <u>conformity</u>.

_____

_____ 15. The <u>hormonal</u> changes of adolescence have some effect on mood swings.

_____

DIRECTIONS Write three words or phrases to describe each term given.

16. cliques _____

17. crowds _____

18. peer pressure _____

19. sturm und drang _____

20. relationships with parents _____

Adolescence

READING THE SECTION
DIRECTIONS Read each sentence and fill in the blank with the correct word or phrase.

1. Erik Erikson labeled one key aspect of adolescent development an identity

   _____. **(crisis/moratorium)**

2. James Marcia concluded that there are four categories of identity

   _____, or reaction patterns and processes. **(diffusion/status)**

3. Adolescents experiencing identity _____ seem to be constantly search for meaning in life. **(diffusion/achievement)**

4. Identity _____ is the category in which adolescents have coped with crises and explored options. **(diffusion/achievement)**

5. Adolescents in the identity _____ category make a commitment to shut out other possibilities. **(moratorium/foreclosure)**

DIRECTIONS Read each of the following descriptions, and write who or what is "speaking" in the space provided.

_____ 6. "I represent a turning point in a person's development."

_____ 7. "I am the identity status category in which students have explored options."

_____ 8. "I am the category in which adolescents have not committed themselves to personal beliefs or an occupational path."

_____ 9. "I am the category in which teens delay making commitments about important questions."

_____ 10. "I am the category in which adolescents make a commitment that forecloses other possibilities."

POST-READING QUICK CHECK
DIRECTIONS In your own words, write the definition of each term.

11. identity crisis: _____

_____

12. identity status: _____

_____

13. identity foreclosure: _____

_____

14. identity diffusion: _____

_____

DIRECTIONS Use vocabulary terms to write a summary of what you
learned in the section.

_____

_____

_____

_____

_____

Adolescence

READING THE SECTION

DIRECTIONS Read the definitions below. In the space provided, write the letter of the term that matches each definition.

_____ 1. offenses that are illegal only when they are committed by minors

_____ 2. disorder characterized by self-starvation

_____ 3. disorder characterized by binge eating

_____ 4. the use of alcohol and drugs to alter mood, done to the point of damage

_____ 5. illegal activities committed by children or adolescents

a. anorexia nervosa

b. bulimia nervosa

c. juvenile delinquency

d. status offenses

e. substance abuse

DIRECTIONS In the space provided, write the vocabulary term that best matches each description.

_____ 6. a life-threatening eating disorder characterized by a distorted body image

_____ 7. symptoms may include addiction, aggressive behavior, accidents, impaired judgment, physical symptoms of specific diseases caused by different drugs such as nicotine or alcohol

_____ 8. a life threatening eating disorder characterized by dramatic measures to eliminate food, such as vomiting

_____ 9. the most extreme examples of this behavior includes robbery, rape, and homicide, which are crimes regardless of the offender's age

_____ 10. examples of these activities include truancy, drinking, smoking, and running away from home

POST-READING QUICK CHECK

DIRECTIONS On the line provided before each statement, write **T** if a statement is true and **F** if a statement is false. If the statement is false, write the correct term on the line after each sentence that makes the sentence a true statement.

_____ 11. Adolescents with <u>anorexia nervosa</u> usually weigh less than 85 percent of what would be considered a healthy weight.

_____

_____ 12. The great majority of people who suffer from <u>bulimia nervosa</u> are female.

_____

_____ 13. Symptoms of <u>substance abuse</u> include excessive dieting and exercise, excessive weight loss, and obsession with food.

_____

_____ 14. The term <u>juvenile delinquency</u> refers to offenses such as truancy.

_____

_____ 15. The term <u>status offenses</u> refers to activities that are illegal regardless of age.

_____

DIRECTIONS Answer the questions on the lines provided.

16. What factors contribute to teenage pregnancy?

_____

_____

17. What are some of the factors that contribute to juvenile delinquency?

_____

_____

Adolescence

Applying What You've Learned

Peer Pressure

Can you resist peer pressure and stand up for your beliefs even if it means risking an awkward situation or confrontation?

1. INTRODUCTION
First, read through the simulation in your textbook. Then use this worksheet to help you complete the simulation in your textbook.

2. SIMULATION OVERVIEW
When conducting this simulation, you may wish to clarify your thinking about some of its essential components. Before beginning the simulation, complete the graphic organizer below to help you generate specific ideas about dialogue, characters, and peer pressure situations.

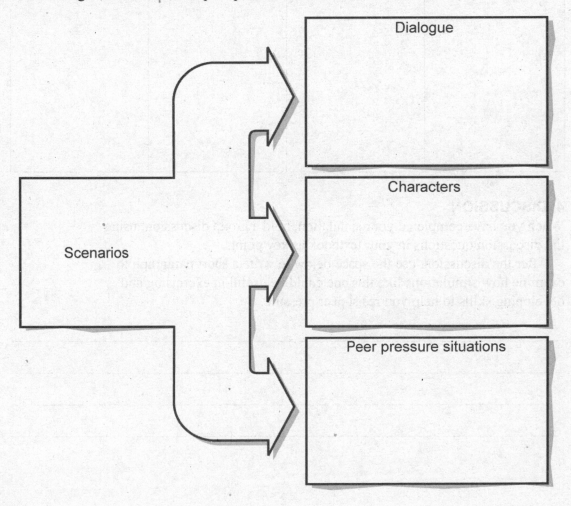

3. SIMULATION EXTENSION

You can practice your refusal skills by thinking of more peer pressure situations. Record those situations in the first column of the chart below. Then decide which refusal skill you would use and write it in the appropriate column.

Peer pressure situations	Refusal Skills		
	Blame someone else	**Suggest something else to do**	**Give a reason**

4. DISCUSSION

When you have completed your simulation, hold a group discussion, using the discussion questions in your textbook as key points.

After the discussion, use the space below to write a short paragraph to examine how simulations like this one could be useful in exercising and developing skills to help you resist peer pressure.

_____

_____

_____

_____

Adulthood

Guided Reading

Section 1

READING THE SECTION

DIRECTIONS Read the definitions below. In the space provided, write the letter of the term that matches each definition.

_____ 1. goals and achievements associated by Erik Erikson with young adulthood

_____ 2. the financial consequences of this event are more severe for women than for men

_____ 3. a system in which men play the dominant role in marriage and society

_____ 4. the concept of who a person is and what he or she stands for in terms of values

_____ 5. a period in the lives of people in their 20s when they reevaulate the decisions and choices they have made

a. identity

b. patriarchy

c. developmental tasks

d. reassessment

e. divorce

DIRECTIONS On the line provided before each statement, write **T** if a statement is true and **F** if a statement is false. If the statement is false, write the correct term on the line after each sentence that makes the sentence a true statement.

_____ 6. Beginning a career or job is one of the <u>developmental tasks</u> associated with young adulthood.

_____

_____ 7. A period of <u>reassessment</u> may bring about major life changes.

_____

_____ 8. An important part of young adulthood is the development of <u>patriarchy</u>, a sense of who you are and what you stand for.

_____

_____ 9. <u>Identity</u> is part of the history of marriage.

_____

_____ 10. <u>Reassessment</u> has many financial and emotional costs.

_____

POST-READING QUICK CHECK

DIRECTIONS Read each sentence and fill in the blank with the correct word or phrase.

11. The _____ rate rose steadily throughout most of the last century before leveling off in the 1980s. **(divorce/reassessment)**

12. Throughout history, _____ have changed according to the needs of people and society. **(children of divorce/marriage practices)**

13. The financial impact of _____ on women is less severe than it used to be. **(identity/divorce)**

14. When people ask themselves, "Why am I doing this?" this is an example of

    _____. **(reassessment/identity)**

15. As the system of _____ has changed, spouses are more likely to be considered equal partners. **(divorce/patriarchy)**

DIRECTIONS In your own words, write the definition of each term.

16. identity: _____

    _____

17. patriarchy: _____

    _____

18. marriage practices: _____

    _____

19. divorce: _____

    _____

Adulthood

READING THE SECTION

DIRECTIONS Read each of the following descriptions, and write who or what is "speaking" in the space provided.

_____ 1. "I am the feeling of emptiness and loss mothers and father feel when children leave home."

_____ 2. "I am the period in middle adulthood when people's perspectives change in a major way."

_____ 3. "I am the ability to create, originate, and produce."

_____ 4. "I am the end of menstruation that occurs in a woman's late 40s or early 50s."

_____ 5. "I am the second period of reassessment often triggered by a midlife transition."

DIRECTIONS Read the definitions below. In the space provided, write the letter of the term that matches each definition.

_____ 6. young adult children who, after leaving home, return to live with their parents

_____ 7. period of searching in midlife that resembles adolescence

_____ 8. many myths surround this major life change that women experience in their late 40s or early 50s

_____ 9. the focus of these activities is improving one's quality of life and strengthening relationships

_____ 10. people born between 1946 and 1964

a. developmental tasks

b. middlescence

c. baby boomers

d. boomerang generation

e. menopause

POST-READING QUICK CHECK

DIRECTIONS On the line provided before each statement, write **T** if a statement is true and **F** if a statement is false. If the statement is false, write the correct term on the line after each sentence that makes the sentence a true statement.

_____ 11. <u>Generativity</u> is a period in middle adulthood when people's perspectives change in a major way.

_____

_____ 12. <u>Midlife crisis</u> is a period of searching in adulthood that in some ways resembles the search of adolescence.

_____

_____ 13. The <u>baby boomers</u> were born in the years beginning just after World War II and extending to 1946.

_____

_____ 14. <u>Midlife transition</u> is a feeling of loss experienced by parents when their children have left home to establish their own lives.

_____

_____ 15. <u>Generativity</u> is the end of menstruation that usually occurs in women in their late 40s or early 50s.

_____

DIRECTIONS Write three words or phrases to describe each term given.

16. generativity _____

17. midlife transition _____

18. midlife crisis _____

19. empty-nest syndrome _____

20. menopause _____

Adulthood

READING THE SECTION

DIRECTIONS Read each sentence and fill in the blank with the correct word or phrase.

1. _____ are developmental theories that maintain that aging is the result of genetics. (**Programmed theories/Cellular damage theories**)

2. _____ are unstable elements in our bodies that some scientists think cause damage to our bodies. (**Dementia/Free radicals**)

3. According to the view called _____, proteins within a cell bind together, toughening body tissue and causing aging. (**cross-linking/senile dementia**)

4. _____ is a progressive form of mental deterioration that affects about 10 percent of people over 65. (**Alzheimer's disease/Ego integrity**)

5. _____ occurs after the age of 65. (**Senile dementia/ Cross-linking**)

DIRECTIONS Read each of the following descriptions, and write who or what is "speaking" in the space provided.

_____ 6. "I am a serious loss of cognitive functioning characterized by memory loss."

_____ 7. "I believe that life is meaningful and worthwhile even when physical abilities are not what they used to be."

_____ 8. "I believe that cells malfunction as a result of damage, not heredity."

_____ 9. "I am an unstable molecule that can cause damage to the body."

_____ 10. "I believe that aging is the result of genetics."

POST-READING QUICK CHECK

DIRECTIONS Look at each set of four terms. On the line provided, write
the letter of the term that does not relate to the others.

_____ 11. a. programmed theories
               b. aging is caused by genetics
               c. cells malfunction because of
                  damage
               d. biological clock moves at
                  predetermined pace

_____ 12. a. cellular damage theories
               b. aging result of genetics
               c. cells malfunction because of
                  damage
               d. free radicals

_____ 13. a. successful aging
               b. dementia
               c. ego integrity
               d. positive outlook

_____ 14. a. tasks of late adulthood
               b. adjusting to physical change
               c. adjusting to illness
               d. choosing a career

DIRECTIONS Use vocabulary terms to write a summary of what you
learned in the section.

_____

_____

_____

_____

_____

Adulthood

READING THE SECTION

DIRECTIONS Read the definitions below. In the space provided, write the letter of the term that matches each definition.

_____ 1. Elisabeth Kubler-Ross's theory that people pass through phases in dealing with a terminal illness

_____ 2. a homelike place where dying people and their families are given physical and emotional support

_____ 3. mourning over someone precious who has been taken away

_____ 4. a legal document intended to spare people the indignity and cost of being kept alive when there is no hope of survival

_____ 5. physician-assisted suicide for terminally-ill and long suffering patients, illegal in most states

a. hospice

b. euthanasia

c. living will

d. bereaved

e. stages of dying

DIRECTIONS In the space provided, write the vocabulary term that best matches each description.

_____ 6. a speech praising the person who has just died

_____ 7. denial and bargaining are two of the phases

_____ 8. unlike hospitals, they do not restrict visiting hours

_____ 9. many people support making this procedure legal

_____ 10. many people write them to avoid being kept alive by artificial support

POST-READING QUICK CHECK

DIRECTIONS On the line provided before each statement, write **T** if a statement is true and **F** if a statement is false. If the statement is false, write the correct term on the line after each sentence that makes the sentence a true statement.

_____ 11. A <u>funeral</u> is a traditional way for a community to acknowledge that one of its members has died.

_____

_____ 12. People who are <u>angry</u> may have feelings of sadness, loneliness, numbness, and even relief.

_____

_____ 13. The <u>stages of dying</u> include anger and acceptance.

_____

_____ 14. <u>Hospitals</u> do not restrict visiting hours and deal exclusively with patients who have terminal illnesses.

_____

_____ 15. A <u>living will</u> does not go into effect until a person is incapacitated.

_____

DIRECTIONS Answer the questions on the lines provided.

16. What are the stages of dying?

_____

_____

17. What are some of the elements involved in dying with dignity?

_____

_____

Adulthood

Applying What You've Learned

Experiencing the Stages of Adulthood

What would you like to say to your future self? How might you see yourself looking back as an older adult?

1. INTRODUCTION
First, read through the simulation in your textbook. Then use this worksheet to help you complete the simulation in your textbook.

2. GENERATE IDEAS
Discuss what you have learned with your group. Then use the table below to record your ideas about what life might be like in young, middle, and late adulthood.

Independence	Marriage, Divorce, Children	Career	Generativity, Midlife Crisis, Empty-nest Syndrome	Physical, Cognitive, Social Changes

3. WRITE THE LETTERS

After you have completed your letters, compare the letter you wrote to
your future self with the letter you wrote to your younger self in reply.
Record your observations in the Venn diagram below. In the left circle, list
only those issues that concern you as a younger person. In the right circle,
list only those issues that you think will concern you as an older person. In
the center, where the circles overlap, list the issues that concern you both
as a young adult and an older adult.

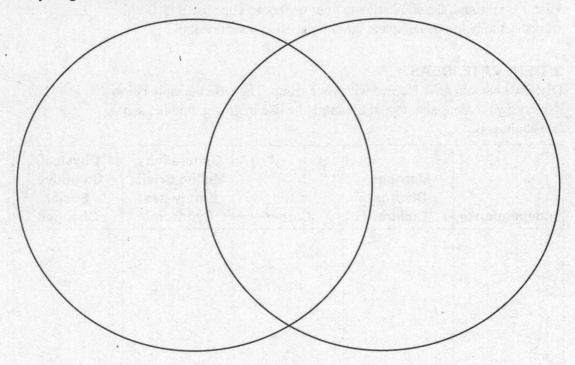

4. SHARE AND DISCUSS THE LETTERS

Read the discussion questions in your textbook, then refer back to the notes
you took during your group discussion. Discuss your ideas and the
conclusions that you can draw with the rest of the class.

After the class discussion, use the space below to write a short paragraph
to explain the process of aging, that is, moving through the phases of
adulthood from young adulthood through middle adulthood to late
adulthood.

_____

_____

_____

_____

Motivation and Emotion   Guided Reading

READING THE SECTION

DIRECTIONS Read the definitions below. In the space provided, write the letter of the term that matches each definition.

_____ 1. behavior patterns genetically transmitted from generation to generation

_____ 2. a stimulus that moves a person to behave in ways designed to accomplish a specific goal

_____ 3. a tendency to maintain a state of equilibrium in the body

_____ 4. the forces that motivate an organism to take action

_____ 5. a condition in which we require something we lack

a. motive

b. need

c. drives

d. instincts

e. homeostasis

DIRECTIONS On the line provided before each statement, write **T** if a statement is true and **F** if a statement is false. If the statement is false, write the correct term on the line after each sentence that makes the sentence a true statement.

_____ 6. According to <u>drive-reduction theory</u>, people and animals experience a drive arising from a need as an unpleasant tension.

_____

_____ 7. <u>Self-actualization</u> refers to the need to become what one is capable of being.

_____

_____ 8. The behavior patterns genetically transmitted from generation to generation are known as <u>drives</u>.

_____

_____ 9. A <u>need</u> is a stimulus that moves a person to behave in ways designed to accomplish a specific goal.

_____

_____ 10. <u>Homeostasis</u> works like a thermostat.

_____

POST-READING QUICK CHECK
DIRECTIONS Read each sentence and fill in the blank with the correct word or phrase.

11. Instinct, drive-reduction, humanistic, and sociocultural are the leading theories of

_____. **(behavior/motivation)**

12. Maslow claimed that people strive to fulfill their capacity for

_____. **(self-actualization/homeostasis)**

13. Biological needs and psychological needs give rise to _____. **(instincts/drives)**

14. Abraham Maslow devised a _____ to organize human requirements that may be lacking. **(hierarchy of needs/self-actualization)**

15. _____ are sometimes called fixed-action patterns. **(Needs/Instincts)**

DIRECTIONS In your own words, write the definition of each term.

16. need: _____

_____

17. motive: _____

_____

18. drive: _____

_____

19. instinct: _____

_____

Motivation and Emotion

READING THE SECTION

DIRECTIONS Read each of the following descriptions, and write who or what is "speaking" in the space provided.

_____ 1. "I am the 'start eating center' in the brain."

_____ 2. "I am the condition in which people weigh 30 percent more than their recommended weight."

_____ 3. "I am the part of the brain involved in the regulation of body temperature and various aspects of psychological motivation."

_____ 4. "I am one of the factors that plays a major role in causing obesity."

_____ 5. "I am a basic biological drive that is regulated by both biological and psychological factors."

DIRECTIONS Read the definitions below. In the space provided, write the letter of the term that matches each definition.

_____ 6. in addition to heredity, I also play a role in obesity

_____ 7. ability to keep alive or sustain with nourishment

_____ 8. part of the brain that functions as a "stop-eating" center

_____ 9. part of the brain that functions as a "start-eating" center

_____ 10. applies to more than six out of ten adult Americans

a. obese

b. sustain

c. lateral hypothalamus

d. ventromedial hypothalamus

e. psychological factors

POST-READING QUICK CHECK

DIRECTIONS On the line provided before each statement, write **T** if a statement is true and **F** if a statement is false. If the statement is false, write the correct term on the line after each sentence that makes the sentence a true statement.

_____ 11. Information about blood sugar level is communicated to the <u>hypothalamus,</u> which is involved in the regulation of body temperature and psychological motivation and emotion.

_____

_____ 12. Certain people with a particular gene may not receive the biological signal that they have eaten enough to <u>sustain</u> them.

_____

_____ 13. Both heredity and psychological factors are <u>causes of weight loss</u>.

_____

_____ 14. The mouth, the stomach, and the hypothalamus all play a role in the <u>hunger drive</u>.

_____

_____ 15. The <u>lateral hypothalamus</u> is the "stop-eating" center of the brain.

_____

DIRECTIONS Write three words or phrases to describe each term given.

16. hunger drive _____

17. causes of obesity_____

18. hypothalamus _____

19. lateral hypothalamus _____

20. ventromedial hypothalamus _____

Motivation and Emotion　　　　　　　Guided Reading

READING THE SECTION
DIRECTIONS Read each sentence and fill in the blank with the correct word or phrase.

1. People who are driven to get ahead are said to have high

   _____. **(stimulus motives/achievement motivation)**

2. _____ include sensory stimulation, activity, exploration, and manipulation of the environment. **(Extrinsic rewards/Stimulus motives)**

3. According to _____, people need to organize their perceptions, opinions, and beliefs in a harmonious manner. **(intrinsic rewards/balance theory)**

4. _____ is the desire to join with others and be part of something larger than oneself. **(Affiliation/Cognitive consistency)**

5. _____ include good grades and a good income. **(Extrinsic rewards/Intrinsic rewards)**

DIRECTIONS Read each of the following descriptions, and write who or what is "speaking" in the space provided.

_____ 6. "I am the state or condition in which people experience an absence of stimulation."

_____ 7. "I am the theory that believes people want their thoughts and attitudes to be consistent with their actions."

_____ 8. "I satisfy learning goals with qualities such as self-satisfaction."

_____ 9. "I motivate people to think and behave in a way that fits what they believe and how others expect them to think and behave."

_____ 10. "I sometimes cause irritability, boredom, and even hallucinations in experiment participants."

POST-READING QUICK CHECK

DIRECTIONS Look at each set of four terms. On the line provided, write the letter of the term that does not relate to the others.

_____ 11. a. stimulus motives
        b. intrinsic rewards
        c. sensory stimulation
        d. sensory deprivation

_____ 13. a. sensory stimulation
        b. cognitive consistency
        c. balance theory
        d. cognitive-dissonance theory

_____ 12. a. achievement motivation
        b. extrinsic rewards
        c. intrinsic rewards
        d. sensory deprivation

_____ 14. a. affiliation
        b. Stanley Schachter
        c. adolescence
        d. intrinsic rewards

DIRECTIONS Use vocabulary terms to write a summary of what you learned in the section.

_____

_____

_____

_____

_____

Motivation and Emotion

Guided Reading

Section 4

READING THE SECTION

DIRECTIONS Read the definitions below. In the space provided, write the letter of the term that matches each definition.

_____ 1. James-Lange, Cannon-Bard, and cognitive appraisal are examples

_____ 2. states of feeling

_____ 3. a feeling that tends to be between the extremes of happiness or sadness

_____ 4. these often express the six basic emotions

_____ 5. emotions often come in pairs, with one emotion being followed by its opposite

a. emotions

b. opponent-process theory

c. facial expressions

d. neutral

e. theories of emotions

DIRECTIONS In the space provided, write the vocabulary term that best matches each description.

_____ 6. anger, disgust, fear, happiness, sadness, and surprise are included under this heading

_____ 7. positive ones make life worth living and negative ones make life difficult

_____ 8. theory that emotions follow behavior and that people can change their feelings by changing their behavior

_____ 9. theory that emotions are triggered by external stimuli and that emotions and bodily responses occur simultaneously

_____ 10. theory originated by Richard Solomon that emotions tend to be experienced in pairs of opposites

POST-READING QUICK CHECK

DIRECTIONS On the line provided before each statement, write **T** if a statement is true and **F** if a statement is false. If the statement is false, write the correct term on the line after each sentence that makes the sentence a true statement.

_____ 11. <u>Emotions</u> are states of feeling that can be positive, negative, or neutral.

_____

_____ 12. <u>Body language</u> expresses six basic emotions.

_____

_____ 13. The <u>cognitive appraisal</u> theory of emotions, developed by Richard Solomon, states that emotions often come in pairs.

_____

_____ 14. The Cannon-Bard theory of emotions states that emotions are triggered by external stimuli and occur at the same time as bodily responses.

_____

_____ 15. The <u>James-Lange</u> theory of emotions argues that people label their emotions based on their cognitive appraisal of the situation.

_____

DIRECTIONS Answer the questions on the lines provided.

16. What does the World Database of Happiness do?

_____

_____

17. What are some of the components of emotions?

_____

_____

Motivation and Emotion   Applying What You've Learned

Identifying Motivations and Emotions

What can you learn about motivation and emotion through developing fictional characters?

1. INTRODUCTION
First, read through the simulation in your textbook. Then use this worksheet to help you complete the simulation in your textbook.

2. DEFINING THE CHARACTERS
Before you begin to act out your scenarios, use the chart below to create a biography for each of your characters. Record the information that you will use in creating the characters that you will be portraying. At the bottom of each column, speculate about what feelings and emotions might be motivating them.

	Mark (Student)	Tish (Mother)	Robert (Father)	Shelly (Admissions Officer)
Name				
Age				
Education				
Background				
Possible motivations				

3. ACTING OUT THE SCENARIOS

After you have created a biography for each of your characters, break up
into the groups organized by your teacher. Use the questions provided in
the textbook to help you brainstorm to understand the characters better.
Record the results of your brainstorming in the chart below.

Mark	Tish	Robert	Shelly

Based on your brainstorming, what answers did you come up with to the
questions in the textbook? Use the space provided to note your conclusions
about the exercise.

_____

_____

_____

_____

4. DISCUSSION

Discuss the characters and their feelings after all the scenarios are acted
out. What motives, needs, and drives can you identify? Did the arguments
in the scenario fit into Maslow's hierarchy of needs? Once the discussion is
completed, jot down your conclusions on the lines below.

_____

_____

_____

_____

Theories of Personality

READING THE SECTION

DIRECTIONS Read the definitions below. In the space provided, write the letter of the term that matches each definition.

_____ 1. an aspect of personality that is considered to be relatively stable

_____ 2. people who tend to be active, self-expressive, and gain energy from other people

_____ 3. the patterns of feelings, motives, and behavior that set people apart

_____ 4. many psychologists consider these to be the basic factors or dimensions of personality

_____ 5. people who tend to be imaginative and to look inward

a. personality

b. trait

c. introverts

d. extroverts

e. five-factor model

DIRECTIONS On the line provided before each statement, write **T** if a statement is true and **F** if a statement is false. If the statement is false, write the correct term on the line after each sentence that makes the sentence a true statement.

_____ 6. Extroverts tend to look inward rather than to other people for ideas.

_____

_____ 7. Eysenck's five-factor model relates to the personality types identified by Hippocrates.

_____

_____ 8. Introverts and extroverts are at opposite poles.

_____

_____ 9. Hippocrates, Gordon Allport, and Hans J. Eysenck can all be considered trait theorists.

_____

_____ 10. A trait is an aspect of personality.

_____

 Reading and Activity Workbook

POST-READING QUICK CHECK

DIRECTIONS Read each sentence and fill in the blank with the correct word or phrase.

11. Psychologists study _____ to learn about the feelings, motives, and behavior that set one person apart from another. **(personality/introverts)**

12. The _____ has been used to study driving habits and political beliefs. **(five-factor model/trait approach)**

13. Hans J. Eysenck devised a system of _____ in an attempt to better understand personality. **(five factors/personality dimensions)**

14. Talkativeness, assertiveness, and activity characterize _____. **(extroverts/introverts)**

15. The ideas of Hippocrates bear a certain resemblance to the ideas of the trait theorist

_____. **(Hans J. Eysenck/Gordon Allport)**

DIRECTIONS In your own words, write the definition of each term.

16. personality: _____

_____

17. trait: _____

_____

18. introverts: _____

_____

19. extroverts: _____

_____

Theories of Personality   Guided Reading

Section 2

READING THE SECTION
DIRECTIONS Read each of the following descriptions, and write who or
what is "speaking" in the space provided.

_____ 1. "I am the psychological structure in the mind that
represents reason and good sense."

_____ 2. "I embody ideas and images of the experience of all
human beings."

_____ 3. "I am the defense mechanism that uses self-deception to
justify unacceptable behaviors or ideas."

_____ 4. "I send my impulses outward on to other people, seeing
my faults in other people."

_____ 5. "I remove anxiety-causing ideas from consciousness by
pushing them into the unconscious."

DIRECTIONS Read the definitions below. In the space provided, write
the letter of the term that matches each definition.

_____ 6. an individual under stress returns to behavior   a. id
characteristic of an earlier stage of
development   b. defense mechanisms

_____ 7. feelings of inadequacy and insecurity   c. regression

_____ 8. methods the ego uses to avoid recognizing   d. collective unconscious
ideas or emotions that may cause anxiety
e. inferiority complex

_____ 9. psychological structure in the mind that
represents basic drives such as hunger

_____ 10. a store of human concepts shared by all
people across all cultures

POST-READING QUICK CHECK

DIRECTIONS On the line provided before each statement, write **T** if a statement is true and **F** if a statement is false. If the statement is false, write the correct term on the line after each sentence that makes the sentence a true statement.

_____ 11. The <u>superego</u> incorporates the standards and values of the community and provides us with our moral sense.

_____

_____ 12. <u>Regression</u> removes anxiety-causing ideas from consciousness.

_____

_____ 13. <u>Rationalization</u> is a defense mechanism.

_____

_____ 14. <u>Sigmund Freud</u> developed the concept of archetypes.

_____

_____ 15. Alfred Adler developed the concept of the <u>collective unconscious</u>.

_____

DIRECTIONS Write three words or phrases to describe each term given.

16. defense mechanisms _____

17. ego _____

18. archetypes _____

19. inferiority complex _____

20. Freud's stages of personality development _____

Theories of Personality   Guided Reading

READING THE SECTION
DIRECTIONS Read each sentence and fill in the blank with the correct
word or phrase.

1. The process called _____ is one in which people learn the
   socially desirable behaviors of their culture. **(socialization/behaviorism)**

2. According to _____, personality is shaped and learning
   acquired by the interaction of several factors. **(social cognition theory/socialization)**

3. According to the social cognitive model, personal, behavioral, and environmental

   factors shape _____. **(behaviorism/personal development)**

4. According to social-learning theorists, _____also influence
   how we act in certain situations. **(internal variables/external forces)**

5. The founder of _____claimed that external forces or influences
   largely shape people's behavior. **(learning theory/behaviorism)**

DIRECTIONS Read each of the following descriptions, and write who or
what is "speaking" in the space provided.

_____ 6. "In my 1948 novel *Walden Two*, I described a utopian
                          society in which people are happy and content."

_____ 7. "I conducted a famous experiment known as the Bobo
                          Doll study."

_____ 8. "I am limited in my ability to explain personality
                          because I do not describe or explain inner human
                          experience."

_____ 9. "In the 1930s, I took up Watson's ideas and emphasized
                          the effects of reinforcement on behavior."

_____ 10. "Social-learning theory, like behaviorism, does not pay
                          enough attention to the role I play in determining
                          individual differences in behavior."

POST-READING QUICK CHECK

DIRECTIONS Look at each set of four terms. On the line provided, write the letter of the term that does not relate to the others.

_____ 11. a. behaviorism
              b. Albert Bandura
              c. John Watson
              d. B. F. Skinner

_____ 13. a. internal variables
              b. goals
              c. self-efficacy expectations
              d. behaviorism

_____ 12. a. social cognitive theory
              b. Albert Bandura
              c. socialization
              d. Bobo Doll study

_____ 14. a. personal factors
              b. environmental factors
              c. social cognitive theory
              d. socialization

DIRECTIONS Use vocabulary terms to write a summary of what you learned in the section.

_____

_____

_____

_____

_____

Theories of Personality

READING THE SECTION

DIRECTIONS Read the definitions below. In the space provided, write the letter of the term that matches each definition.

_____ 1. focuses on the roles that ethnicity, gender, socioeconomic status, and culture play in shaping personality and behavior

_____ 2. consistency between one's self-concept and one's experience

_____ 3. a view of oneself as an individual

_____ 4. process of adapting to a new or different culture

_____ 5. focuses on self-awareness, self-fulfillment, and ethical conduct

a. self-concept

b. congruence

c. acculturation

d. humanistic psychology

e. sociocultural psychology

DIRECTIONS In the space provided, write the vocabulary term that best matches each description.

_____ 6. according to this scheme, there are physiological, security, social, esteem, and self-actualization needs

_____ 7. Carl Rogers placed great emphasis on the ability to view oneself as an individual

_____ 8. these sorts of people tend to define themselves in terms of the groups to which they belong and often give priority to the goals of their groups

_____ 9. the path to this state requires getting in touch with our genuine feelings and acting on them

_____ 10. Western capitalist society fosters this trait or characteristic in people

POST-READING QUICK CHECK

DIRECTIONS On the line provided before each statement, write **T** if a statement is true and **F** if a statement is false. If the statement is false, write the correct term on the line after each sentence that makes the sentence a true statement.

_____ 11. The process of <u>congruence</u> is undergone by people who come to the United States from other countries.

_____

_____ 12. People from Asia or Africa tend to be more <u>individualistic</u> in their attitudes and actions.

_____

_____ 13. <u>Acculturation</u> is the process of adapting to a new or different culture.

_____

_____ 14. Humanistic psychologists are separated from lower animals because they recognize a desire to achieve <u>self-actualization</u>, to reach their full potential.

_____

_____ 15. Carl Rogers, an advocate of <u>humanistic psychology</u>, believed that people are basically good and mentally healthy.

_____

DIRECTIONS Answer the questions on the lines provided.

16. What are the five levels of Maslow's hierarchy of needs?

_____

_____

17. According to sociocultural psychology, what factors shape personality and behavior?

_____

_____

Theories of Personality   Applying What You've Learned
                                                              Lab

Your Self: Applying Theories of Personality

Can theories of personality explain what makes you unique?

1. INTRODUCTION
First, read through the lab in your textbook. Then use this worksheet to help you complete the lab in your textbook.

2. PROFILING YOUR PERSONALITY
Use the graphic organizer below to take notes about how each of the four theories that you have chosen might apply to your personality. Use each quarter of the circle to make notes about how that theory would view your characteristic features and traits. Make notes as well about images that might be used to illustrate that region of your collage.

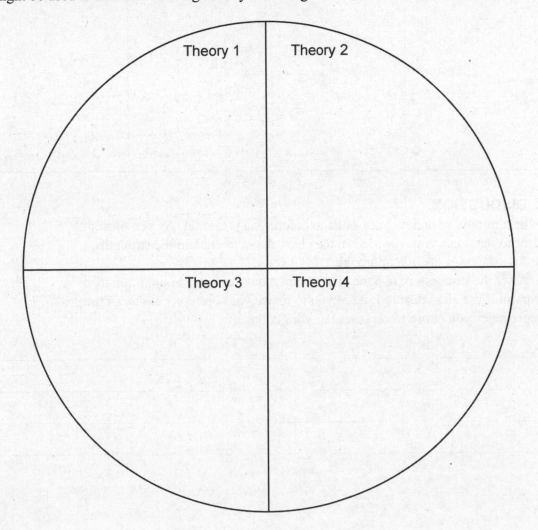

3. CREATING AND PRESENTING YOUR COLLAGE

Use the chart below to organize the presentation of your collage. Make notes in each column about the ways in which that approach seems relevant as a means of describing your personality. Provide reasons why and how you chose the approach that you think best describes your personality. Also, provide details about why the other three approaches did not seem as on target as your first choice.

Favored Approach	Different Approaches		
	Second Approach	Third Approach	Fourth Approach

4. DISCUSSION

Take a minute to review your collage before you present it. As you present, refer to the notes you recorded in the chart above to explain the strengths and weaknesses of each approach.

After the discussion, use the space below to write a short paragraph to explain if the class discussion led you to revise your opinions of any of the approaches you chose to represent in your collage.

_____

_____

_____

_____

Psychological Tests

Guided Reading

Section 1

READING THE SECTION
DIRECTIONS Read the definitions below. In the space provided, write the letter of the term that matches each definition.

_____ 1. a group of test items that suggest whether or not the test taker is answering honestly

_____ 2. established standards of performance

_____ 3. what people say about their attitudes, feelings, and behavior

_____ 4. systematic means of recording the frequency with which certain behaviors occur

_____ 5. administered and scored the same way every time

a. behavior rating scales

b. self-reports

c. standardized test

d. validity scales

e. norms

DIRECTIONS On the line provided before each statement, write **T** if a statement is true and **F** if a statement is false. If the statement is false, write the correct term on the line after each sentence that makes the sentence a true statement.

_____ 6. In designing a test, test makers use a <u>norm group</u> in administering the test to a large group of people who are similar to those for whom the test is intended.

_____

_____ 7. <u>Validity scales</u> are used to measure behavior in classrooms and schools.

_____

_____ 8. <u>Behavior rating scales</u> involve questions that, if answered in a certain way, let the psychologist know the test taker is not answering honestly.

_____

_____ 9. Psychologists and educators are trained in how to administer and score <u>standardized tests</u> accurately.

_____

_____ 10. Most psychological tests rely on people's <u>norms</u>, that is, what people say about themselves.

_____

POST-READING QUICK CHECK

DIRECTIONS Read each sentence and fill in the blank with the correct word or phrase.

11. Psychologists use _____ to measure behavior in classrooms and hospitals. **(behavior-rating scales/validity scales)**

12. Stanford-Binet and Wechsler are examples of _____. **(norms/standardized tests)**

13. _____ are established standards of behavior designed to tell test administrators which scores are low, average, or high. **(validity scales/norms)**

14. A _____ is a group of test takers similar to those for whom the test is intended. **(norm group/social group)**

DIRECTIONS In your own words, write the definition of each term.

15. self-reports: _____

_____

16. norms: _____

_____

17. behavior-rating scales: _____

_____

18. standardized test: _____

_____

Psychological Tests

Guided Reading

Section 2

READING THE SECTION
DIRECTIONS Read each of the following descriptions, and write who or
what is "speaking" in the space provided.

_____ 1. "I measure people's skills and the knowledge they have
in specific academic areas."

_____ 2. "I am used to determine whether a person is likely to do
well in a given field of work or study."

_____ 3. "I help people determine whether their interests are
similar to those of people in various lines of work."

_____ 4. "I force the test taker to choose an answer, even if none
seems to fit precisely."

_____ 5. "I am intended to measure a person's ability to do well
in college."

DIRECTIONS Read the definitions below. In the space provided, write
the letter of the term that matches each definition.

_____ 6. for example, test takers are asked to indicate
which of a group of activities they like most
and which they like least

_____ 7. tests that measure a narrow range of skills

_____ 8. one example is the Kuder Preference
Records

_____ 9. the Law School Admission Test and the
Medical School Admission Test are
examples

_____ 10. a general aptitude test used in college
admissions

a. achievement tests

b. aptitude tests

c. vocational interest
inventories

d. forced-choice format

e. SAT

POST-READING QUICK CHECK

DIRECTIONS On the line provided before each statement, write **T** if a statement is true and **F** if a statement is false. If the statement is false, write the correct term on the line after each sentence that makes the sentence a true statement.

_____ 11. A history test is an example of an <u>aptitude test</u>.

_____

_____ 12. The Law School Admission Test is an example of an <u>achievement test</u>.

_____

_____ 13. The Strong-Campbell Interest Inventory is an example of a <u>vocation interest inventory</u>.

_____

_____ 14. The Kuder Career Search test has a <u>forced-choice format</u>.

_____

_____ 15. The <u>SAT</u> used to be called the Scholastic Assessment Test.

_____

DIRECTIONS Write three words or phrases to describe each term given.

16. achievement tests _____

17. aptitude tests _____

18. vocational interest inventories _____

19. forced-choice format _____

20. SAT _____

Psychological Tests

Guided Reading

Section 3

READING THE SECTION

DIRECTIONS Read each sentence and fill in the blank with the correct word or phrase.

1. _____ present test takers with a standardized group of test items in the form of a questionnaire. **(Objective tests/Projective tests)**

2. _____ have no clearly specified answers. **(Objective tests/ Projective tests)**

3. Projective tests use a(n) _____. **(questionnaire/ open-ended format)**

4. The _____ is an example of an objective test. **(California Psychological Inventory/Rorschach Inkblot Test)**

5. The _____ is an example of a projective test. **(Minnesota Multiphasic Personality Inventory/Thematic Apperception Test)**

DIRECTIONS Read each of the following descriptions, and write who or what is "speaking" in the space provided.

_____ 6. "I devised a test that asks people to tell me what a drawing or inkblot looks like."

_____ 7. "I was developed by Henry Murray and Christiana Morgan in the 1930s to get people to tell stories that reveal their needs and values."

_____ 8. "I am the test that is most widely used in clinical work and research that requires measurement of personality traits."

_____ 9. "I was designed to measure 15 'normal' personality traits, such as dominance, sociability, responsibility, and tolerance."

_____ 10. "I present 567 items in a true-false format."

POST-READING QUICK CHECK

DIRECTIONS Look at each set of four terms. On the line provided, write the letter of the term that does not relate to the others.

_____ 11. a. objective tests
         b. Minnesota Multiphasic
             Personality Inventory
         c. California Psychological
             Inventory
         d. Rorschach Inkblot Test

_____ 12. a. projective tests
         b. Thematic Apperception Test
         c. California Psychological
             Inventory
         d. Rorschach Inkblot Test

DIRECTIONS Use vocabulary terms to write a summary of what you learned in the section.

_____

_____

_____

_____

_____

Psychological Tests

Guided Reading

Section 4

READING THE SECTION

DIRECTIONS Read the definitions below. In the space provided, write the letter of the term that matches each definition.

_____ 1. must be wary of items that use absolutes such as *all*, *always*, or *never*

_____ 2. must consider every possible choice

_____ 3. preparing hastily for an exam

_____ 4. must answer in brief but complete sentences

_____ 5. consciously changing the thoughts one has in a particular situation

a. cognitive restructuring

b. cramming

c. multiple-choice questions

d. true-false questions

e. short-answer questions

DIRECTIONS In the space provided, write the vocabulary term that best matches each description.

_____ 6. commonly used in standardized tests such as the SAT

_____ 7. can be reduced by being prepared, by overlearning, and by thinking helpful thoughts

_____ 8. in taking this kind of test, you should express your strongest ideas first

_____ 9. identifying self-defeating thoughts and replacing them with positive messages is part of this method

_____ 10. studying a reasonable amount of time every day is more effective than using this method the night before a big test

POST-READING QUICK CHECK

DIRECTIONS On the line provided before each statement, write **T** if a statement is true and **F** if a statement is false. If the statement is false, write the correct term on the line after each sentence that makes the sentence a true statement.

_____ 11. When answering a <u>multiple-choice question</u>, you should look for answers that are opposite, for one of them is often the correct choice.

_____

_____ 12. In <u>true-false questions</u>, items that are longer and provide more information than others tend to be true.

_____

_____ 13. <u>Cramming</u> is an excellent way to prepare the night before a test.

_____

_____ 14. <u>Cognitive restructuring</u> in the context of a test means imagining yourself in a different, less stressful situation, such as playing golf.

_____

_____ 15. <u>Overlearning</u> means studying to the point where you are unable to distinguish between main ideas and supporting details.

_____

DIRECTIONS Answer the questions on the lines provided.

16. What are some ways of coping with test anxiety?

_____

_____

17. What are some tips for taking tests?

_____

_____

Psychological Tests Applying What You've Learned

Lab

Writing a Personality Quiz

What do your answers to questions on a personality quiz say about you?
Can your answers reveal your gender?

1. INTRODUCTION
First, read through the lab in your textbook. Then use this worksheet to
help you complete the lab in your textbook.

2. WRITING THE QUIZ
Use the chart below to help you write fifteen questions for a personality
quiz. From this group of fifteen, you will choose the five best questions.
The first column lists a variety of categories or topics. Use the space in the
second column to write a question that asks something about that topic.

Topic	Question
Animals	
Trees	
Colors	
Leisure-time activities	
Playing sports	
Reality TV shows	
Movies	
Music	
Vacation spots	
Clothes	
Computers	
iPods	
Cars	
Nascar	
Hunting & fishing	

3. CLASS PRESENTATION

After you have written the questions and the group has chosen the top five,
write your answers to the questions on the lines below.

1. _____

2. _____

3. _____

4. _____

5. _____

4. WRITTEN PRESENTATION

Answer all fifteen of the questions that your group came up with. Then use
the lines below to write a paragraph about how the answers to these
questions do or do not reveal your gender. Explain why some are more
revealing than others.

_____

_____

_____

_____

5. DISCUSSION

Use the answers to the questions proposed for discussion in the textbook to
create a list of changes you might make in designing a future quiz to reveal
gender. Write down the ideas you come up with on the lines below.

_____

_____

_____

_____

Gender Roles

Guided Reading

Section 1

READING THE SECTION

DIRECTIONS Read the definitions below. In the space provided, write the letter of the term that matches each definition.

_____ 1. fixed and oversimplified beliefs about the ways in which men and women ought to behave

_____ 2. small and getting smaller, and these variations are between groups, not individuals

_____ 3. societal expectations about how males and females should behave

_____ 4. the sex of an individual, male or female

_____ 5. affectionate care

a. gender

b. gender roles

c. gender stereotypes

d. nurturance

e. gender differences

DIRECTIONS On the line provided before each statement, write **T** if a statement is true and **F** if a statement is false. If the statement is false, write the correct term on the line after each sentence that makes the sentence a true statement.

_____ 6. Gender roles define appropriate and normal masculine and feminine behavior in a particular culture.

_____

_____ 7. Gender stereotypes are fixed and oversimplified beliefs about how men and women ought to behave.

_____

_____ 8. Women tend to exceed men in trust and aggression.

_____

_____ 9. Men are more swayed than women by physical appearance in mate selection.

_____

_____ 10. Nurturance has been linked to high levels of testosterone.

_____

POST-READING QUICK CHECK

DIRECTIONS Read each sentence and fill in the blank with the correct word or phrase.

11. In mate selection, women place a higher value than men on

    _____. **(physical appearance/dependability)**

12. _____ are fixed and oversimplified beliefs about how men and women ought to behave. **(Gender roles/Gender stereotypes)**

13. Girls seem to acquire _____ faster than boys.
    (language skills/spatial ability)

14. The fact that men talk less than women about feelings represents a difference in

    _____. **(cognitive differences/**

    communication styles differences)

15. Possibly the most fundamental physical characteristic of any human being is his or

    her _____. **(gender/hair and eye color)**

DIRECTIONS In your own words, write the definition of each term.

16. gender: _____

    _____

17. gender roles: _____

    _____

18. gender stereotypes: _____

    _____

19. nurturance: _____

    _____

Gender Roles

Guided Reading

Section 2

READING THE SECTION

DIRECTIONS Read each of the following descriptions, and write who or what is "speaking" in the space provided.

_____ 1. "I am the specialization of the two sides of the brain that occurs during fetal development."

_____ 2. "I am the process by which social learning can occur through observation and imitation of others."

_____ 3. "I am the process of gender role development."

_____ 4. "I am the cluster of ideas about physical qualities, behaviors, and personality traits associated with one sex or the other."

_____ 5. "I am the theory that says boys and girls identify with their same-sex parent and learn gender roles from them."

DIRECTIONS Read the definitions below. In the space provided, write the letter of the term that matches each definition.

_____ 6. process by which children learn about both male and female gender role behavior by observing males and females with whom they interact

_____ 7. this begins to take place at a very early age and various theories, which fall into two major categories, have been proposed to explain it

_____ 8. these include psychoanalytic theory, social-learning theory, and gender-schema theory

_____ 9. these focus on genetics and hormones in the development of gender-related behavior

_____ 10. theory which holds that gender is such a strong force in our society that children come to organize their perceptions along gender lines

a. gender typing

b. psychological views of gender typing

c. modeling

d. gender schema

e. biological views of gender typing

POST-READING QUICK CHECK

DIRECTIONS On the line provided before each statement, write **T** if a statement is true and **F** if a statement is false. If the statement is false, write the correct term on the line after each sentence that makes the sentence a true statement.

_____ 11. <u>Modeling</u> occurs during fetal development and may occur differently in boys and girls.

_____

_____ 12. The <u>genetic</u> theory of gender typing says that the genes that determine sex also determine gendered behavior.

_____

_____ 13. A <u>lateralization</u> is a cluster of ideas about the physical qualities, behaviors, and personality traits associated with both sexes.

_____

_____ 14. The <u>social-learning theory</u> says that gender differences are modeled by parents and reinforced by positive and negative reactions.

_____

_____ 15. The specialization of two sides of the brain is called <u>lateralization</u>.

_____

DIRECTIONS Write three words or phrases to describe each term given.

16. gender typing _____

17. lateralization _____

18. modeling _____

19. gender schema _____

20. theories to explain gender typing _____

Gender Roles

READING THE SECTION

DIRECTIONS Read each sentence and fill in the blank with the correct word or phrase.

1. In a famous work of _____, Margaret Mead explored how gender roles vary from culture to culture. **(ethnography/archaeology)**

2. The ancient _____ may have given rise to the myth of the Amazons. **(Egyptians/Scythians)**

3. Research has shown that _____ can vary from culture to culture. **(biology/gender roles)**

4. _____ over time have included political leaders, factory workers, celebrities, politicians, and tradeworkers. **(Women's roles/ Roles restricted to women)**

5. Margaret Mead was an _____ who explored the issue of variation in gender roles from culture to culture. **(anthropologist/archaeologist)**

DIRECTIONS Read each of the following descriptions, and write who or what is "speaking" in the space provided.

_____ 6. "I studied three different groups of people—the Mundugumor, the Arapesh, and the Tchambuli."

_____ 7. "I am the study of human cultures."

_____ 8. "I may vary from person to person and culture to culture."

_____ 9. "I was a politician, attorney, and supreme court justice."

_____ 10. "I am the queen of England who died in 1603."

POST-READING QUICK CHECK

DIRECTIONS Look at each set of four terms. On the line provided, write the letter of the term that does not relate to the others.

_____ 11. a. Margaret Mead
           b. ethnography
           c. Mundugumor
           d. Scythians

_____ 13. a. Egypt
           b. Assyria
           c. United States
           d. Akkad

_____ 12. a. Mundugumor
           b. Scythians
           c. Arapesh
           d. Tchambuli

_____ 14. a. Abraham Lincoln
           b. Queen Elizabeth I
           c. Sarah Bernhardt
           d. Sandra Day O'Connor

DIRECTIONS Use vocabulary terms to write a summary of what you learned in the section.

_____

_____

_____

_____

_____

Applying What You've Learned

Identifying Gender Stereotypes

How accurate are gender stereotypes? If you saw an actor portray an anonymous character, do you think that you could tell whether the character was supposed to be a man or a woman? Here's a chance to find out.

1. INTRODUCTION
First, read through the simulation in your textbook. Then use this worksheet to help you complete the simulation in your textbook.

2. INITIAL PREPARATION
Before you begin to create your scenarios, use the chart below to brainstorm a number of gendered roles. Record details about the characters' personalities and situations. These details will enable the class to guess your characters' genders. Your small group can use the notes in the chart to write descriptions on note cards or paper.

	Character 1	Character 2	Character 3	Character 4	Character 5
Name					
Age					
Education					
Background					
Career					

Applying What You've Learned

3. CREATING, PRESENTING, AND OBSERVING THE SCENARIOS

Use the chart below to make notes about important points to remember as you work with your partner. Note any steps that you and your partner might take to successfully complete your scenario.

Showcase the main aspects of gender type	Provide a number of gender clues	Write out a basic script	Practice your script

In the space below, record your observations of the presentations made by other groups. Note the identifying markers that helped you to identify gender roles. Remember to look for both traditional and nontraditional clues.

_____

_____

_____

_____

4. DISCUSSION

After all the scenarios have been presented, discuss both stereotypical and nontraditional gender roles. Once the discussion is over, jot down your conclusions on the lines below.

_____

_____

_____

_____

Stress and Health

Guided Reading
Section 1

READING THE SECTION
DIRECTIONS Read the definitions below. In the space provided, write
the letter of the term that matches each definition.

_____ 1. a response linked to intense pressure that can
         have psychological and physical effects

      a. stress

      b. distress

_____ 2. least stressful type because the choices are
         positive

      c. stressor

_____ 3. the arousal of one's mind and body in
         response to demands made upon them

      d. approach-approach
         conflict

_____ 4. a single goal can produce opposite motives

      e. approach-avoidance
         conflict

_____ 5. an event or situation that produces stress

DIRECTIONS On the line provided before each statement, write **T** if a
statement is true and **F** if a statement is false. If the statement is false, write
the correct term on the line after each sentence that makes the sentence a
true statement.

_____ 6. A kind of positive stress called <u>distress</u> can increase sharpness and
         motivation.

         _____

_____ 7. People in <u>avoidance-avoidance conflict</u> are forced to choose the lesser of two
         evils.

         _____

_____ 8. <u>Approach-avoidance conflict</u> involves a choice between alternatives that have
         both good and bad aspects.

         _____

_____ 9. The <u>type A</u> personality is laid-back and relaxed.

         _____

_____ 10. There are <u>four</u> types of conflict that have been identified as sources of stress.

         _____

POST-READING QUICK CHECK

DIRECTIONS Read each sentence and fill in the blank with the correct word or phrase.

11. Psychologists think that _____ can keep people alert and involved. **(distress/eustress)**

12. _____ can strain people's ability to adjust to various situations. **(Distress/Eustress)**

13. Choosing between cake and ice cream is an example of an

    _____ conflict. **(approach-avoidance/approach-approach)**

14. Going to the dentist or letting a toothache get worse is an example of an

    _____ conflict. **(approach-approach/avoidance-avoidance)**

15. Deciding whether to buy a new DVD player that would cost a lot of money is an

    example of an _____ conflict. **(approach-approach/**

    approach-avoidance)

DIRECTIONS In your own words, write the definition of each term.

16. stress: _____

    _____

17. distress: _____

    _____

18. eustress: _____

    _____

19. types of conflict: _____

    _____

Stress and Health

Guided Reading

Section 2

READING THE SECTION

DIRECTIONS Read each of the following descriptions, and write who or what is "speaking" in the space provided.

_____ 1. "I am the beliefs people have that they can accomplish goals that they set for themselves."

_____ 2. "I am the response that mobilizes the body for defensive action."

_____ 3. "I am the body's similar response to different sources of stress."

_____ 4. "I am the personality characteristic that commitment, challenge, and control all contribute to."

_____ 5. "I am one of the three stages, besides the alarm reaction and the resistance stage, that makes up the general adaptation syndrome."

DIRECTIONS Read the definitions below. In the space provided, write the letter of the term that matches each definition.

_____ 6. alarm reaction that mobilizes the body when a person perceives a stressor

_____ 7. the alarm reaction, resistance stage, and exhaustion stage make up this response

_____ 8. prevents disease by producing white blood cells that destroy disease-causing microorganisms

_____ 9. these beliefs are closely related to self-confidence and boost people's abilities to withstand stress

_____ 10. these include self-efficacy expectations, psychological hardiness, humor, predictability, and social support

a. self-efficacy expectation

b. general adaptation syndrome

c. responses to stress

d. fight-or-flight reaction

e. the immune system

POST-READING QUICK CHECK

DIRECTIONS On the line provided before each statement, write **T** if a statement is true and **F** if a statement is false. If the statement is false, write the correct term on the line after each sentence that makes the sentence a true statement.

_____ 11. <u>Psychological hardiness</u> is made up of commitment, challenge, and control.

_____

_____ 12. During the <u>alarm reaction</u> of GAS, people attempt to find a way to cope with the stressor to avoid being overwhelmed by negative reactions.

_____

_____ 13. Stress can contribute to the suppression of the <u>general adaptation syndrome</u>.

_____

_____ 14. The exhaustion stage is part of <u>psychological hardiness</u>.

_____

_____ 15. <u>Stress</u> has serious effects on the immune system.

_____

DIRECTIONS Write three words or phrases to describe each term given.

16. self-efficacy expectation _____

17. general adaptation syndrome _____

18. responses to stress _____

19. fight-or-flight reaction _____

20. immune system _____

Stress and Health | **Guided Reading**

Section 3

READING THE SECTION

DIRECTIONS Read each sentence and fill in the blank with the correct word or phrase.

1. _____ headaches usually have a sudden onset and are identified by severe throbbing pain on one side of the head. **(Muscle-tension/ Migraine)**

2. The field of _____ is concerned with the relationship between psychological factors and the prevention and treatment of physical illness. **(health psychology/alternative medicine)**

3. The personality type labeled _____ is prone to distress. **(type B/type D)**

4. _____ uses chemicals to kill diseased cells. **(Alternative medicine/Chemotherapy)**

5. _____ is one form of alternative medicine. **(Acupuncture/Chemotherapy)**

DIRECTIONS Read each of the following descriptions, and write who or what is "speaking" in the space provided.

_____ 6. "I am the type of behavior more likely to be found in people who develop heart disease."

_____ 7. "I am the type of headache that may last for hours or days."

_____ 8. "I explore the various ways in which states of mind influence physical well-being."

_____ 9. "I am the form of alternative medicine that uses massage techniques."

_____ 10. "I am the health problem that both type A and type D personalities are at greater risk of experiencing."

POST-READING QUICK CHECK

DIRECTIONS Look at each set of four terms. On the line provided, write the letter of the term that does not relate to the others.

_____ 11. a. type A behavior
           b. controlling weight
           c. anger and hostility
           d. job strain

_____ 13. a. type D behavior
           b. distress
           c. cardiac risk
           d. relaxed

_____ 12. a. quitting smoking
           b. controlling weight
           c. lack of exercise
           d. reducing hypertension

_____ 14. a. chemotherapy
           b. herbal remedies
           c. acupuncture
           d. reflexology

DIRECTIONS Use vocabulary terms to write a summary of what you learned in the section.

_____

_____

_____

_____

_____

Stress and Health

Guided Reading

Section 4

READING THE SECTION
DIRECTIONS Read the definitions below. In the space provided, write the letter of the term that matches each definition.

_____ 1. these include relaxation techniques and exercise

_____ 2. a way to handle stress that may involve socially unacceptable behavior

_____ 3. involves changing the environment or situation to remove stressors in socially acceptable ways

_____ 4. these include substance abuse and withdrawal

_____ 5. these include denial and projection

a. defensive coping

b. active coping

c. defense mechanisms

d. coping methods

e. defensive methods

DIRECTIONS In the space provided, write the vocabulary term that best matches each description.

_____ 6. aggression and defense mechanisms are two of the four examples of these

_____ 7. in the long run, this form of coping is self-defeating and usually harmful

_____ 8. denial, repression, and projection are three types of these

_____ 9. involves changing one's response to stress so that stressors are no longer harmful

_____ 10. these include changing stressful thoughts and breathing techniques

POST-READING QUICK CHECK

DIRECTIONS On the line provided before each statement, write **T** if a statement is true and **F** if a statement is false. If the statement is false, write the correct term on the line after each sentence that makes the sentence a true statement.

_____ 11. <u>Denial</u> is the removal of anxiety-causing ideas from conscious awareness.

_____

_____ 12. <u>Projection</u> is the refusal to accept the reality of something bad or upsetting.

_____

_____ 13. An example of <u>repression</u> might be a soldier pushing his feelings of anxiety about going into combat into his unconscious.

_____

_____ 14. <u>Aggression</u> often heightens conflict because it can motivate someone to seek revenge.

_____

_____ 15. <u>Meditation</u> is an example of a relaxation technique that involves focusing one's attention on a single point of reference and eliminating other thoughts from the mind.

_____

DIRECTIONS Answer the questions on the lines provided.

16. What are some methods of defensive coping?

_____

_____

17. What are some methods of active coping?

_____

_____

Stress and Health   Applying What You've Learned
                                                                    Simulation

Stress and Active Coping Methods

What is the most effective way to cope with a stressful situation?

1. INTRODUCTION
First, read through the simulation in your textbook. Then use this
worksheet to help you complete the simulation in your textbook.

2. PREPARE THE SIMULATION
Before beginning the simulation, complete the graphic organizer below. Jot
down notes that occur to you about the six kinds of stressful situations.
These notes will help you to come up with specific ideas about the
situation you are assigned to work on. They will also help you to listen
attentively as other simulations are performed.

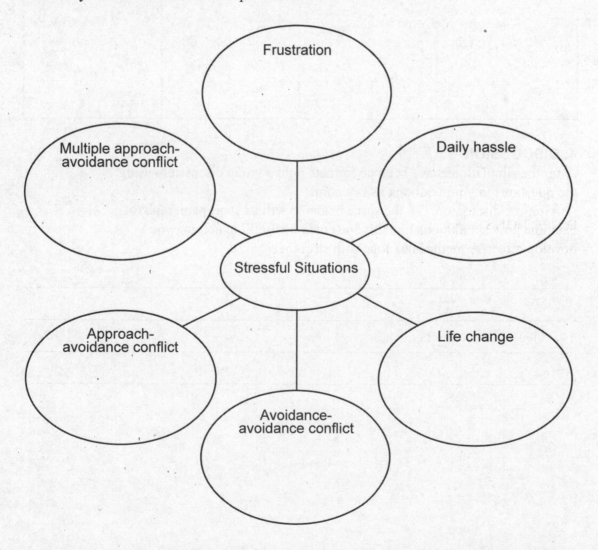

3. PERFORM AND OBSERVE SIMULATIONS

As you watch the other simulations being performed, use the chart below
to take notes on the performances. You will use your notes in the
discussion that follows the simulations.

Stressor or conflict being demonstrated	Notes of an Audience Member		
	Depiction	Coping methods	Other methods

4. DISCUSSION

After the simulations have been performed, hold a group discussion, using
the questions in your textbook as key points.

After the discussion, use the space below to write a short paragraph to
examine how simulations like this one could be useful in helping you
develop effective methods to cope with stress.

_____

_____

_____

_____

Psychological Disorders   Guided Reading

READING THE SECTION

DIRECTIONS Read the definitions below. In the space provided, write the letter of the term that matches each definition.

_____ 1. clusters of symptoms considered diseases only within specific societies

_____ 2. widely used classification system for psychological disorders

_____ 3. standards such as typicality and maladaptivity used to determine psychological disorders

_____ 4. mental processes that cause suffering

_____ 5. include anxiety and depressive disorders

a. psychological disorders

b. culture-bound syndromes

c. major categories of psychological disorders

d. *Diagnostic and Statistical Manual of Mental Disorders*

e. criteria of disorders

DIRECTIONS On the line provided before each statement, write **T** if a statement is true and **F** if a statement is false. If the statement is false, write the correct term on the line after each sentence that makes the sentence a true statement.

_____ 6. The *DSM* is used by psychologists, insurance companies, and researchers.

_____

_____ 7. Typicality describes behavior that impairs an individual's ability to function adequately in everyday life.

_____

_____ 8. Approximately 25 percent of American adults suffer from a mental disorder in a given year.

_____

_____ 9. Somatic symptom disorders is one of the 19 basic categories of psychological disorders.

_____

_____ 10. Culture-bound syndromes are behavior patterns or thoughts that interfere with a person's ability to cope with everyday life.

_____

POST-READING QUICK CHECK

DIRECTIONS Read each sentence and fill in the blank with the correct word or phrase.

11. The normality of behavior is often determined by its _____, or the degree to which it is average for the behavior of the majority. **(typicality/maladaptivity)**

12. _____ that violate a society's accepted norms may also be an indication of a psychological disorder. **(Culture-bound syndromes/ Socially unacceptable behaviors)**

13. Agoraphobia and panic disorder were both classified as _____.

    (depressive disorders/anxiety disorders)

14. _____ disorders involve physical symptoms for which no biological cause can be found. **(Somatic symptom/Impulse control)**

15. Many behaviors associated with _____ would be considered abnormal by people who were unaware of the cultural context. **(psychological disorders/culture-bound syndromes)**

DIRECTIONS In your own words, write the definition of each term.

16. psychological disorders: _____

   _____

17. culture-bound syndromes: _____

   _____

18. maladaptivity: _____

   _____

19. typicality: _____

   _____

Psychological Disorders   Guided Reading

                                                      Section 2

READING THE SECTION

DIRECTIONS Read each of the following descriptions, and write who or what is "speaking" in the space provided.

_____ 1. "I am the fear of being in places or situations where escape may be difficult or impossible."

_____ 2. "I am the persistent feelings of anxiety caused by stressful and traumatic experience."

_____ 3. "I am a disorder that involves cycles of mood changes from depression to elation and back again."

_____ 4. "I am the fear of social situations in which I might be exposed to the scrutiny of others."

_____ 5. "I am irrational, excessive, and persistent fear of spiders."

DIRECTIONS Read the definitions below. In the space provided, write the letter of the term that matches each definition.

_____ 6. word that derives from the Greek word for "fear"

_____ 7. period of extreme excitement characterized by hyperactivity and chaotic behavior

_____ 8. condition that typically involves feelings of helplessness, hopelessness, worthlessness, guilt, and sadness

_____ 9. period of intense fear characterized by shortness of breath, dizziness, rapid heart rate, trembling, sweating, choking, and nausea

_____ 10. unwanted thoughts and actions that occur over and over again

a. phobia

b. panic attack

c. obsessive-compulsive disorder (OCD)

d. depression

e. mania

POST-READING QUICK CHECK

DIRECTIONS On the line provided before each statement, write **T** if a statement is true and **F** if a statement is false. If the statement is false, write the correct term on the line after each sentence that makes the sentence a true statement.

_____ 11. <u>Obsessive-compulsive disorders</u> include post-traumatic stress disorder and acute stress disorder.

_____

_____ 12. <u>Compulsive hoarding</u> is a type of obsessive-compulsive disorder.

_____

_____ 13. <u>Depression</u> involves a cycle of mood changes from depression to elation and back again.

_____

_____ 14. <u>Mania</u> is a period of extreme excitement characterized by hyperactivity and chaotic behavior.

_____

_____ 15. <u>Phobia</u> refers to a persistent, excessive, or irrational fear of an object or situation.

_____

DIRECTIONS Write three words or phrases to describe each term given.

16. post-traumatic stress disorder _____

17. panic attack _____

18. social anxiety _____

19. agoraphobia _____

20. types of anxiety disorders _____

Psychological Disorders   Guided Reading

READING THE SECTION

DIRECTIONS Read each sentence and fill in the blank with the correct word or phrase.

1. The condition called _____ refers to feelings of detachment from one's mental processes or body. (**depersonalization disorder/somatic symptom disorder**)

2. The word _____ refers to the expression of psychological distress through physical symptoms. (**dissociation/somatization**)

3. The term _____ refers to the separation of certain personality components or mental processes from conscious thought. (**depersonalization/dissociation**)

4. _____ refers to a person's unrealistic preoccupation with thoughts of serious disease. (**Conversion disorder/Hypochondriasis**)

5. _____ refers to the experience of a change or loss of physical functioning in a major part of the body for which there is no medical explanation. (**Conversion disorder/Hypochondriasis**)

DIRECTIONS Read each of the following descriptions, and write who or what is "speaking" in the space provided.

_____ 6. "I am the condition in which people have psychological problems but experience inexplicable physical symptoms."

_____ 7. "I am the condition in which people feel outside their bodies, observing themselves at a distance."

_____ 8. "I am the condition of which the most common form is daydreaming."

_____ 9. "I am the condition in which people are sometimes unable to move their legs even though there is no medical explanation for the disability."

_____ 10. "I am the condition in which people become absorbed by minor physical symptoms."

POST-READING QUICK CHECK

DIRECTIONS Look at each set of four terms. On the line provided, write
the letter of the term that does not relate to the others.

_____ 11. a. dissociation   _____ 12. a. somatic symptom disorder
           b. hypochondriasis   b. conversion disorder
           c. amnesia   c. amnesia
           d. fugue   d. hypochondriasis

DIRECTIONS Use vocabulary terms to write a summary of what you
learned in the section.

_____

_____

_____

_____

_____

Psychological Disorders

READING THE SECTION

DIRECTIONS Read the definitions below. In the space provided, write the letter of the term that matches each definition.

_____ 1. include psychoanalytic, psychological, biological, and multifactorial

_____ 2. mental disorder characterized by a loss of contact with reality

_____ 3. have varied over the ages from culture to culture, such as the ancient world, the Muslim world, and the European Middle Ages

_____ 4. includes paranoia and disturbances of movement

_____ 5. an immobile, expressionless, coma-like state

a. schizophrenia

b. catatonic stupor

c. perspectives on schizophrenia

d. perceptions of schizophrenia

e. symptoms of schizophrenia

DIRECTIONS In the space provided, write the word or phrase that best matches each description.

_____ 6. the view of schizophrenia that the ego is overwhelmed by the id and the individual regresses and confuses fantasy with reality

_____ 7. view of schizophrenia that attributes the condition to a loss of synapses in the brain

_____ 8. view of schizophrenia that maintains a family environment that includes pushy, critical parents puts children at risk for the condition

_____ 9. view of schizophrenia that claims both biological and psychological factors combine to put people at risk

_____ 10. perception of schizophrenia that regarded it as a form of witchcraft or possession by demons

POST-READING QUICK CHECK

DIRECTIONS On the line provided before each statement, write **T** if a statement is true and **F** if a statement is false. If the statement is false, write the correct term on the line after each sentence that makes the sentence a true statement.

_____ 11. In early modern Europe, outsiders paid to watch the patients at Bethlem Hospital in London.

_____

_____ 12. In the Enlightenment, doctors took a clinical and humane approach to mental illness based on their reading in the Qur'an.

_____

_____ 13. In the late 1800s, mental disorders were widely seen as a result of the gods' anger.

_____

_____ 14. In the 1930s and 1940s, many schizophrenics were killed in Nazi Germany.

_____

_____ 15. In the Enlightenment, mental illness began to be seen as a disease instead of a crime.

_____

DIRECTIONS Answer the questions on the lines provided.

16. What are the four main perspectives on schizophrenia?

_____

_____

17. What are three major symptoms of schizophrenia?

_____

_____

Psychological Disorders

Guided Reading

Section 5

READING THE SECTION

DIRECTIONS Read each of the following descriptions, and write who or what is "speaking" in the space provided.

_____ 1. "I am the patterns of inflexible traits that disrupt social life or work and distress the individual."

_____ 2. "I am the view that says heredity plays a role in personality disorder."

_____ 3. "I am the feeling of sympathy or understanding of others' feelings."

_____ 4. "I am the type of personality disorder that makes people act in an emotional and dramatic way to gain attention."

_____ 5. "As a narcissistic personality disorder, these are my main characteristics."

DIRECTIONS Read the definitions below. In the space provided, write the letter of the term that matches each definition.

_____ 6. a person with a paranoid personality disorder would be described as typically suspicious and distrustful

_____ 7. in this view, lack of guilt due to a problem in the development of the conscience causes the antisocial personality

_____ 8. an enduring pattern of inner experience that deviates from the expectations of the culture

_____ 9. little of this quality is demonstrated by people with a narcissistic personality

_____ 10. these include schizoid, borderline, and avoidant personalities

a. personality disorders

b. types of personality disorders

c. characteristics of personality disorders

d. perspectives on personality disorders

e. empathy

POST-READING QUICK CHECK

DIRECTIONS On the line provided before each statement, write **T** if a statement is true and **F** if a statement is false. If the statement is false, write the correct term on the line after each sentence that makes the sentence a true statement.

_____ 11. <u>Obsessive-compulsive disorders</u> manifest themselves in an extreme concern with orderliness, perfectionism, and control.

_____

_____ 12. Social inhibitions and feelings of inadequacy are main characteristics of <u>schizoid personality disorders</u>.

_____

_____ 13. The <u>biological view</u> holds that the antisocial personality is caused by a problem in the development of a conscience.

_____

_____ 14. The <u>borderline personality disorder</u> is characterized by instability in interpersonal relationships and self image.

_____

_____ 15. The <u>narcissistic personality disorder</u> is characterized by grandiosity and the need for admiration.

_____

DIRECTIONS Write three words or phrases to describe each term given.

16. personality disorders _____

17. types of personality disorders _____

18. characteristics of personality disorders _____

19. perspectives on personality disorders _____

20. empathy _____

Psychological Disorders   Applying What You've Learned

Diagnosing Psychological Disorders

Can you diagnose a psychological disorder based on a written description of someone's symptoms?

1. INTRODUCTION
First, read through the lab in your textbook. Then use this worksheet to help you complete the lab in your textbook.

2. WRITING THE CASE STUDIES
Before you begin to write your case study, use the chart below to take notes on up to five specific disorders under your assigned general disorder. After you have completed the chart, choose the two disorders for which you have the most extensive notes.

	Case Study 1	Case Study 2	Case Study 3	Case Study 4	Case Study 5
Name					
Age					
Symptoms					
Effect on Life					
Answer (specific disorder)					

3. DIAGNOSING THE DISORDER

Listen carefully as your teacher reads each case study aloud. Use the table below to record your notes about which psychological disorder you think the case study describes and why.

Case Study	Case Study	Case Study	Case Study

For which of the case studies were you able to accurately identify the specific disorder being described? Use the space below to note those you identified and those you did not and why.

_____

_____

_____

_____

4. DISCUSSION

Discuss your conclusions with a group of classmates. How were your conclusions similar? How were they different? As a group, answer the discussion questions in your textbook. After your discussion, use the space below to write a paragraph to explain how being able to interview the people in the case studies might have helped with the diagnosis.

_____

_____

_____

_____

Methods of Therapy Guided Reading

Section 1

READING THE SECTION

DIRECTIONS Read the definitions below. In the space provided, write the letter of the term that matches each definition.

_____ 1. composed of people who share the same problem, such as overeating

_____ 2. psychologically based therapy involving interaction between therapist and client

_____ 3. method of replacing self-defeating attitudes with rational attitudes

_____ 4. method of reducing inappropriate guilt

_____ 5. method to remove obstacles to self-actualization

a. psychotherapy

b. self-help group

c. psychoanalysis

d. humanistic therapy

e. cognitive therapy

DIRECTIONS On the line provided before each statement, write **T** if a statement is true and **F** if a statement is false. If the statement is false, write the correct term on the line after each sentence that makes the sentence a true statement.

_____ 6. <u>Psychologists</u> are medical doctors who can prescribe medication.

_____

_____ 7. <u>Psychiatric social workers</u> counsel people with everyday personal and family problems.

_____

_____ 8. <u>Clinical psychologists</u> must have a doctorate and often work in clinics and hospitals.

_____

_____ 9. <u>Behavior therapy</u> attempts to replace self-defeating attitudes and beliefs with rational, self-enhancing attitudes and beliefs.

_____

_____ 10. <u>Psychiatric nurses</u> are able to dispense but not prescribe medicines.

_____

POST-READING QUICK CHECK
DIRECTIONS Read each sentence and fill in the blank with the correct word or phrase.

11. The goal of _____ is to replace avoidant behavior with coping behavior. **(psychoanalysis/cognitive therapy)**

12. The goal of _____ is to remove obstacles in the path of self-actualization. **(psychoanalysis/humanistic therapy)**

13. The goal of _____ is to replace irrational, self-defeating attitudes and beliefs with rational, self-enhancing attitudes and beliefs. **(cognitive therapy/behavior therapy)**

14. The goal of _____ is to replace maladaptive, self-defeating behavior with adaptive, self-enhancing behavior. **(behavior therapy/ humanistic therapy)**

DIRECTIONS In your own words, write the definition of each term.

15. psychotherapy: _____

_____

16. self-help group: _____

_____

17. psychiatrist: _____

_____

18. Al-Anon: _____

_____

Methods of Therapy

READING THE SECTION

DIRECTIONS Read each of the following descriptions, and write who or what is "speaking" in the space provided.

_____ 1. "I am the process in which the client in psychoanalysis transfers feelings from one person to another."

_____ 2. "I am the hidden meaning in a dream which the therapist interprets."

_____ 3. "I am the primary technique in psychoanalysis in which the analyst asks the client to say whatever comes to his or her mind."

_____ 4. "I was developed in the 1950s by Carl Rogers to help clients find their true selves and realize their potential."

_____ 5. "I am a communication technique in which the listener repeats, rephrases, and asks for clarification."

DIRECTIONS Read the definitions below. In the space provided, write the letter of the term that matches each definition.

_____ 6. the primary goal of this therapy is to help individuals reach their full potential

_____ 7. a term psychoanalysts use to refer to a client's reluctance to discuss issues raised during free association

_____ 8. a method of therapy in which clients are encouraged to take the lead, talking openly about whatever troubles them

_____ 9. the subject matter of a dream as it is remembered by the client

_____ 10. a technique in which the psychoanalyst interprets the content of dreams to unlock thoughts and feelings

a. resistance

b. dream analysis

c. manifest content

d. humanistic therapy

e. nondirective therapy

POST-READING QUICK CHECK

DIRECTIONS On the line provided before each statement, write **T** if a statement is true and **F** if a statement is false. If the statement is false, write the correct term on the line after each sentence that makes the sentence a true statement.

_____ 11. <u>Resistance</u> is a term used to describe a client transferring feelings from one person to another.

_____

_____ 12. <u>Manifest content</u> refers to the hidden meaning of a dream.

_____

_____ 13. <u>Free association</u> is a technique in which a client is encouraged to say whatever comes to his or her mind.

_____

_____ 14. <u>Person-centered therapy</u> was a method of psychotherapy developed by Sigmund Freud.

_____

_____ 15. The primary goal of <u>psychoanalysis</u> is to help individuals reach their full potential.

_____

DIRECTIONS Write three words or phrases to describe each term given.

16. dream analysis _____

17. latent content _____

18. transference _____

19. nondirective therapy _____

20. active listening _____

Methods of Therapy

READING THE SECTION

DIRECTIONS Read each sentence and fill in the blank with the correct word or phrase.

1. _____ is based on Albert Ellis's belief that people are basically logical in their thinking. **(Rational-emotive behavior therapy/Cognitive therapy)**

2. _____ techniques include systematic densensitization and modeling. **(Cognitive therapy/Counterconditioning)**

3. _____ is essentially the opposite of desensitization. **(Behavior therapy/Aversive conditioning)**

4. _____ refers to a series of behaviors that gradually become more like target behavior. **(Successive approximations/Operant conditioning)**

5. A _____ is one in which a therapist sets up a system of rewards. **(desensitization/token economy)**

DIRECTIONS Read each of the following descriptions, and write who or what is "speaking" in the space provided.

_____ 6. "I use techniques such as role-playing and modeling to teach clients to think more realistically."

_____ 7. "I focus on restructuring illogical thought processes, such as arbitrary inference."

_____ 8. "My goal is to end harmful behavior."

_____ 9. "My goal is to encourage adaptive behavior."

_____ 10. "I developed systematic desensitization in the 1950s to treat phobias and other anxiety disorders."

POST-READING QUICK CHECK

DIRECTIONS Look at each set of four terms. On the line provided, write the letter of the term that does not relate to the others.

_____ 11. a. cognitive therapy   _____ 12. a. behavior therapy
            b. Albert Ellis   b. counterconditioning
            c. Aaron Beck   c. Aaron Beck
            d. Joseph Wolpe   d. operant conditioning

DIRECTIONS Use vocabulary terms to write a summary of what you learned in the section.

_____

_____

_____

_____

_____

Methods of Therapy

READING THE SECTION

DIRECTIONS Read the definitions below. In the space provided, write the letter of the term that matches each definition.

_____ 1. also known as electric-shock therapy

_____ 2. also called major tranquilizers, these drugs are often prescribed for schizophrenia

_____ 3. also called minor tranquilizers, these drugs are used as outpatient treatment for panic attacks

_____ 4. used to treat major depressions and sometimes used to treat eating disorders

_____ 5. a compound of a metal used to stabilize patients' moods

a. antianxiety drug

b. antidepressant drug

c. lithium

d. antipsychotic drug

e. electroconvulsive therapy

DIRECTIONS In the space provided, write the vocabulary term that best matches each description.

_____ 6. brain surgery performed to treat psychological disorders

_____ 7. surgical method that involves cutting the nerve pathways in the brain that produces serious side effects such as seizures

_____ 8. these drugs are thought to work by blocking the activity of dopamine in the brain

_____ 9. these drugs work by depressing the activity of the nervous system

_____ 10. these drugs work by increasing the amount of one or both of the neurotransmitters

POST-READING QUICK CHECK

DIRECTIONS On the line provided before each statement, write **T** if a statement is true and **F** if a statement is false. If the statement is false, write the correct term on the line after each sentence that makes the sentence a true statement.

_____ 11. The mineral water used by the Greeks and Romans to treat psychological disorders may have contained <u>lithium</u>.

_____

_____ 12. The Portuguese neurologist Antonio Egas Moniz developed the use of <u>electroconvulsive therapy</u> to treat psychological disorders.

_____

_____ 13. Italian psychiatrists Ugo Cerletti and Lucio Bini pioneered the use of <u>psychosurgery</u> to treat psychological disorders.

_____

_____ 14. The use of <u>antianxiety drugs</u> has enabled many thousands of people with schizophrenia to live outside of mental hospitals.

_____

_____ 15. In 1990 the American Psychiatric Association recommended that <u>electroconvulsive therapy</u> be used primarily for people with major depression who did not respond to drugs.

_____

DIRECTIONS Answer the questions on the lines provided.

16. What are some various types of drug therapy?

_____

_____

17. What are the advantages and disadvantages of electroconvulsive therapy?

_____

_____

Methods of Therapy

Applying What You've Learned

Identifying the Methods of Therapy

As you have seen in the chapter, there are many methods of therapy.
Which approach do you think is best?

1. INTRODUCTION

First, read through the simulation in your textbook. Then use this
worksheet to help you complete the simulation in your textbook.

2. REVIEWING THE METHODS OF THERAPY

Fill out the chart below with a brief description of each method of therapy.
You may wish to conduct additional research in the library or on the
Internet to learn more about each method. You will use these notes when
you choose one specific method to write a skit about.

Method	Terms and Concepts	Goals
Psychoanalysis		
Humanistic therapy		
Person-centered therapy		
Nondirective therapy		
Rational-emotive behavior therapy		
Beck's cognitive therapy		
Counterconditioning		
Operant conditioning		
Drug therapy		
Electroconvulsive therapy		
Psychosurgery		

3. DETERMINING METHODS OF THERAPY BEING SIMULATED

As you observe various simulations, record on the lines below which type
of therapy was being implemented.

1. _____

2. _____

3. _____

4. _____

5. _____

6. _____

7. _____

8. _____

9. _____

10. _____

4. DISCUSSION

In the space below, list which methods of therapy were particularly easy to
identify and which were difficult to guess. Then compare notes with your
classmates in a group discussion.

_____

_____

_____

_____

After the class discussion, use the space below to write a short paragraph to
explain which method of therapy you think is the most effective. Be sure to
give reasons to support your conclusion.

_____

_____

_____

_____

Social Cognition

READING THE SECTION

DIRECTIONS Read the definitions below. In the space provided, write the letter of the term that matches each definition.

_____ 1. conditioning and cognitive evaluation are two of the means by which this takes place

_____ 2. the process by which people weigh evidence and form beliefs on the basis of their judgments of the evidence

_____ 3. beliefs that affect how people behave

_____ 4. strong ones are better predictors of actions than weak ones

_____ 5. persistent beliefs that shape view of the world

a. attitudes

b. cognitive evaluation

c. cognitive anchors

d. ways attitudes develop

e. attitudes and behavior

DIRECTIONS On the line provided before each statement, write **T** if a statement is true and **F** if a statement is false. If the statement is false, write the correct term on the line after each sentence that makes the sentence a true statement.

_____ 6. Advertising relies heavily on <u>cognitive evaluation</u> to shape attitudes.

_____

_____ 7. Parents who praise a child who shares a toy are using <u>conditioning</u> to help shape the child's attitudes.

_____

_____ 8. <u>Cognitive dissonance</u> is an uncomfortable feeling of tension because of a contradiction between attitudes and behaviors.

_____

_____ 9. A person's earliest attitudes serve as <u>observational learnings,</u> or persistent beliefs, that shape the ways in which one sees the world.

_____

_____ 10. The link between attitudes and <u>beliefs</u> is not always strong.

_____

POST-READING QUICK CHECK

DIRECTIONS Read each sentence and fill in the blank with the correct word or phrase.

11. Attitudes are a major aspect of _____. **(social cognition/ animal rescue)**

12. _____ is the process in which people evaluate evidence and form beliefs based on their judgments. **(Observational learning/ Cognitive evaluation)**

13. When children are reinforced and praised for acting in ways that are consistent with

    the attitudes of teachers and parents, this is an example of

    _____. **(conditioning/observational learning)**

14. Most of the time _____ come first and behavior follows. **(actions/attitudes)**

15. _____ tend(s) to keep a person's attitudes from changing. **(Cognitive anchors/Conditioning)**

DIRECTIONS In your own words, write the definition of each term.

16. attitudes: _____

_____

17. cognitive evaluation: _____

_____

18. cognitive anchor: _____

_____

19. cognitive dissonance: _____

_____

Social Cognition

Guided Reading

Section 2

READING THE SECTION
DIRECTIONS Read each of the following descriptions, and write who or what is "speaking" in the space provided.

_____ 1. "I attempt to persuade by arousing loyalty, admiration, desire, or fear rather than by appealing to logic."

_____ 2. "I use evidence and logical arguments to persuade people."

_____ 3. "I am the direct attempt to influence other people's attitudes or views."

_____ 4. "I attempt to persuade people indirectly by associating objects, people, or events with positive or negative cues."

_____ 5. "I am the attitude that makes it easy to turn down requests to buy products or services."

DIRECTIONS Read the definitions below. In the space provided, write the letter of the term that matches each definition.

_____ 6. type of persuasion that presents an argument and then the opposite argument in order to discredit the opposition

_____ 7. these include central route, peripheral route, message, and messenger

_____ 8. relies on evidence and logic

_____ 9. relies on feelings and associations with positive and negative cues

_____ 10. arousing fear is a particularly effective method in this sort of appeal

a. elements of persuasion

b. central route

c. peripheral route

d. two-sides argument

e. emotional appeal

POST-READING QUICK CHECK

DIRECTIONS On the line provided before each statement, write **T** if a statement is true and **F** if a statement is false. If the statement is false, write the correct term on the line after each sentence that makes the sentence a true statement.

_____ 11. The <u>message</u> plays an important role in the peripheral route.

_____

_____ 12. Research shows that <u>persuasion</u>, the repeated exposure to a stimulus, results in a more favorable attitude toward the stimulus.

_____

_____ 13. The use of <u>glittering generalities</u> in a political message is meant to promote positive feelings about the candidate.

_____

_____ 14. People possessing <u>emotional appeals</u> have no trouble turning down various sales appeals.

_____

_____ 15. There are two basic routes of <u>persuasion</u>.

_____

DIRECTIONS Write three words or phrases to describe each term given.

16. persuasion _____

17. central route _____

18. peripheral route _____

19. two-sided argument _____

20. emotional appeal _____

Social Cognition

READING THE SECTION

DIRECTIONS Read each sentence and fill in the blank with the correct word or phrase.

1. The attitude called _____ refers to generalized feelings toward a specific group of people. **(prejudice/discrimination)**

2. A _____ is an individual or group that is blamed for the problems of others. **(scapegoat/immigrant)**

3. _____ refers to the unfair treatment of individuals because they are members of a particular group. **(Discrimination/Social learning)**

4. _____ refers to people who are victims of prejudice and then sometimes discriminate against people who are worse off than themselves. **(Scapegoating/Victimization)**

5. _____ is one way of fighting prejudice. **(Protesting hate crimes/Minding one's own business)**

DIRECTIONS Read each of the following descriptions, and write who or what is "speaking" in the space provided.

_____ 6. "I am the group that approximately 60 percent of the American people think make the crime situation worse."

_____ 7. "I am the word that literally means *prejudgment*."

_____ 8. "I am a member of the group that probably experienced the most extreme form of scapegoating."

_____ 9. "I am the way in which children can acquire attitudes from their parents, including prejudices."

_____ 10. "I am the unfair treatment of individuals because of who they are."

POST-READING QUICK CHECK

DIRECTIONS Look at each set of four terms. On the line provided, write the letter of the term that does not relate to the others.

_____ 11. a. causes of prejudice
　　　　　b. tolerance
　　　　　c. victimization
　　　　　d. scapegoating

_____ 12. a. overcoming prejudice
　　　　　b. speaking up
　　　　　c. exaggerating differences
　　　　　d. protesting hate crimes

DIRECTIONS Use vocabulary terms to write a summary of what you learned in the section.

_____

_____

_____

_____

_____

Social Cognition

Guided Reading

Section 4

READING THE SECTION
DIRECTIONS Read the definitions below. In the space provided, write the letter of the term that matches each definition.

_____ 1. the tendency of people to form opinions of others on the basis of first impressions

_____ 2. people tend to attribute success to themselves and failure to the circumstances

_____ 3. the ways in which people perceive one another

_____ 4. people tend to attribute the behavior of others to internal factors and their own behavior to external factors

_____ 5. the tendency of people to change their opinions of others based on recent interactions rather than first impressions

a. social perception

b. primacy effect

c. recency effect

d. actor-observer bias

e. self-serving bias

DIRECTIONS In the space provided, write the vocabulary term that best matches each description.

_____ 6. the view that people tend to explain behavior in terms of either personality factors or situational factors

_____ 7. the tendency to overestimate the effect of dispositional causes for another's behavior and underestimate situational causes

_____ 8. a personal and sometimes unreasoned judgment

_____ 9. physical contact, eye contact, and cultural considerations are all a part of this

_____ 10. fundamental attribution error, actor-observer bias, and self-serving bias are all a part of this

POST-READING QUICK CHECK

DIRECTIONS On the line provided before each statement, write **T** if a statement is true and **F** if a statement is false. If the statement is false, write the correct term on the line after each sentence that makes the sentence a true statement.

_____ 11. <u>Touching</u> is one way in which people communicate nonverbally.

_____

_____ 12. There is considerable cultural variation in <u>self-serving bias</u>.

_____

_____ 13. When an individual blames other people or the situation for his or her failures, this is an example of <u>actor-observer bias</u>.

_____

_____ 14. The <u>recency effect</u> occurs when people change their opinions of others based on recent interactions.

_____

_____ 15. <u>Social perception</u> refers to the way in which people perceive one another.

_____

DIRECTIONS Answer the questions on the lines provided.

16. What are some elements of attribution theory?

_____

_____

17. What are some aspects to consider in nonverbal communication?

_____

_____

Social Cognition

Guided Reading

Section 5

READING THE SECTION

DIRECTIONS Read each of the following descriptions, and write who or what is "speaking" in the space provided.

_____ 1. "I am the mutual exchange of feelings or attitudes."

_____ 2. "I am the feelings of romantic and sexual attraction."

_____ 3. "I am the process by which people are drawn to others who appeal to them in a number of ways."

_____ 4. "I am the components of love, including passion, intimacy, and commitment."

_____ 5. "I am the idea that people tend to choose as friends and partners those similar to themselves in attractiveness."

DIRECTIONS Read the definitions below. In the space provided, write the letter of the term that matches each definition.

_____ 6. closeness and caring

_____ 7. often done in intricate patterns to accentuate a person's beauty

_____ 8. large eyes, high cheekbones, narrow jaws

_____ 9. a couple's recognition that they are "in love" and want to be together

_____ 10. theory developed by Robert Sternberg to explain the relationships of people in love

a. commitment

b. intimacy

c. triangular model

d. scarification

e. universals of beauty

POST-READING QUICK CHECK

DIRECTIONS On the line provided before each statement, write **T** if a statement is true and **F** if a statement is false. If the statement is false, write the correct term on the line after each sentence that makes the sentence a true statement.

_____ 11. The <u>Yanomamo</u> people of South America beautify themselves with polished sticks.

_____

_____ 12. In the Heian period in <u>Africa</u> women whitened their faces with rice powder.

_____

_____ 13. According to the <u>matching hypothesis</u>, we are more attracted to people who are similar to us.

_____

_____ 14. <u>Attraction</u> refers to the situation in which the person we like likes us back.

_____

_____ 15. The <u>Maya</u> of Central America used boards and straps to flatten the foreheads of infants.

_____

DIRECTIONS Write three words or phrases to describe each term given.

16. intimacy _____

17. passion _____

18. commitment _____

19. matching hypothesis _____

20. perceptions of beauty _____

Social Cognition

Applying What You've Learned

Types of Persuasion

Can you correctly predict whether central or peripheral route persuasion is more effective?

1. INTRODUCTION
First, read through the experiment in your textbook. Then use this worksheet to help you complete the experiment in your textbook.

2. CREATING THE ADS
Use the table below to record your notes as you use the experimental method in examining the two basic routes of persuasion.

Observing	Forming Hypotheses	Testing Hypotheses	Analyzing Data	Evaluating Results

Experiment *continued*   Applying What You've Learned

3. COMPARISON

Use the Venn diagram below to record the advantages of each route, the central route and the peripheral route, as determined by your group discussion.

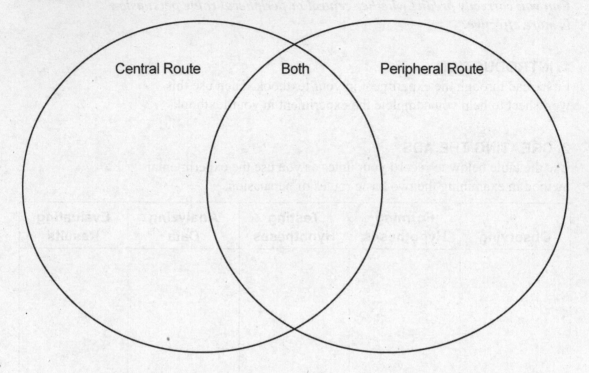

4. DISCUSSION

Read the discussion questions in your textbook, then refer back to the notes you took on the experimental method as you were creating the ads. Discuss your conclusions with the rest of the class.

After the class discussion, use the space below to write a short paragraph to explain which method you think would generally be more effective in creating ads.

_____

_____

_____

_____

Social Interaction

Guided Reading

Section 1

READING THE SECTION
DIRECTIONS Read the definitions below. In the space provided, write
the letter of the term that matches each definition.

_____ 1. the tendency for people to feel less
responsible for a task when the effort is
shared by a group

_____ 2. the concept that people often perform better
when other people are watching

_____ 3. the concern about the opinion of others that
may improve performance

_____ 4. the tendency for people to take greater risks
as part of a group

_____ 5. when people are working together toward a
common goal, they may not try as hard

a. social facilitation

b. evaluation apprehension

c. social loafing

d. diffusion of
responsibility

e. risky shift

DIRECTIONS On the line provided before each statement, write **T** if a
statement is true and **F** if a statement is false. If the statement is false, write
the correct term on the line after each sentence that makes the sentence a
true statement.

_____ 6. Social decision schemes are rules that govern group decision-making.

_____

_____ 7. The strengthening of a group's shared attitudes is called social facilitation.

_____

_____ 8. Democratic leaders exert absolute control over all decisions for the group.

_____

_____ 9. Authoritarian leaders encourage group members to discuss ideas and make
their own decisions.

_____

_____ 10. Laissez-faire leaders take a less active role than democratic leaders.

_____

POST-READING QUICK CHECK

DIRECTIONS Read each sentence and fill in the blank with the correct word or phrase.

11. In the _____ scheme, the group agrees to a decision that was initially supported by a majority of group members. **(majority-wins/first-shift)**

12. In the _____ scheme, the members of a group realize one option is better than others after they learn more about the different choices. **(two-thirds-majority/truth-wins)**

13. In the _____ scheme, groups concur with a decision after about 66 percent of their members come to an agreement about the correct choice. **(majority-wins/two-thirds-majority)**

14. In the _____ scheme, if one person changes his or her mind, others may change to the opposite side as well. **(first-shift/truth-wins)**

DIRECTIONS In your own words, write the definition of each term.

15. social loafing: _____

_____

16. social facilitation: _____

_____

17. evaluation apprehension: _____

_____

18. diffusion of responsibility: _____

_____

Social Interaction

READING THE SECTION

DIRECTIONS Read each of the following descriptions, and write who or what is "speaking" in the space provided.

_____ 1. "I am the pressure to modify one's attitudes and behavior to make them consistent with those of other people."

_____ 2. "I am the standards of behavior that people share."

_____ 3. "I am the tendency for people to give in to major demands once they have given in to minor ones."

_____ 4. "I am unspoken, unwritten rules such as modes of dress or ways of greeting."

_____ 5. "I am spoken or written rules, such as traffic rules and school dress codes."

DIRECTIONS Read the definitions below. In the space provided, write the letter of the term that matches each definition.

_____ 6. people who are protected from the consequences of their actions are more likely to follow orders

_____ 7. people have been trained since childhood to obey authority figures

_____ 8. people have a tendency to give in to major demands once they've given in to major ones

_____ 9. when people are protected from the consequences of their actions this goes up and when they are not sheltered this goes down

_____ 10. people become muddled in their beliefs if they are disturbed by what is happening around them

a. socialization

b. foot-in-the-door effect

c. confusion about attitudes

d. buffers

e. compliance

POST-READING QUICK CHECK

DIRECTIONS On the line provided before each statement, write **T** if a statement is true and **F** if a statement is false. If the statement is false, write the correct term on the line after each sentence that makes the sentence a true statement.

_____ 11. <u>Implicit norms</u> are spoken or written rules.

_____

_____ 12. <u>Explicit norms</u> are unspoken, unwritten rules.

_____

_____ 13. <u>Social norms</u> are the standards of behavior that people share.

_____

_____ 14. <u>Socialization</u> means people have become confused about their beliefs.

_____

_____ 15. <u>Buffers</u> protect people from the consequences of their actions and make them more likely to follow orders.

_____

DIRECTIONS Write three words or phrases to describe each term given.

16. conform _____

17. foot-in-the-door effect _____

18. buffers _____

Social Interaction

Guided Reading

Section 3

READING THE SECTION
DIRECTIONS Read each sentence and fill in the blank with the correct
word or phrase.

1. _____ refers to words or actions that are intended to hurt other
   people. **(Altruism/Aggression)**

2. _____ refers to an unselfish concern for the welfare of other
   people. **(Altruism/Aggression)**

3. The _____ refers to the fact that people are less likely to help
   when other bystanders are present. **(bystander effect/biological view)**

4. _____ is the venting of aggressive impulses.
   (Altruism/Catharsis)

5. The _____ view of aggression maintains that such behavior is
   influenced by people's values, perceptions, and choices. **(psychoanalytic/cognitive)**

DIRECTIONS Read each of the following descriptions, and write who or
what is "speaking" in the space provided.

_____ 6. "My view argues that the brain and hormones are
                             primarily responsible for aggression."

_____ 7. "My view believes that when aggressive behavior is
                             reinforced, people learn to behave aggressively."

_____ 8. "My view holds that repressed aggressive urges might be
                             expressed indirectly."

_____ 9. "My view maintains that the United States is a good
                             example of a country that promotes competition and
                             aggression."

_____ 10. "My view states that people act aggressively because
                              they believe that aggression is justified and necessary."

POST-READING QUICK CHECK
DIRECTIONS Look at each set of four terms. On the line provided, write the letter of the term that does not relate to the others.

_____ 11. a. biological view   _____ 13. a. sociocultural view
          b. hypothalamus   b. hormones
          c. catharsis   c. U.S. promotes competition
          d. testosternone   d. Japan promotes cooperation

_____ 12. a. psychoanalytic view   _____ 14. a. altruism
          b. Freud   b. fear of blunder
          c. testoserone   c. empathy
          d. catharsis   d. competence

DIRECTIONS Use vocabulary terms to write a summary of what you learned in the section.

_____

_____

_____

_____

_____

Social Interaction

Applying What You've Learned
Experiment

Revisiting Milgram

Stanley Milgram conducted his studies of obedience in the 1960s and 1970s. Are Milgram's studies still relevant in the world of the 21st century?

1. INTRODUCTION
First, read through the experiment in your textbook. Then use this worksheet to help you complete the experiment in your textbook.

2. DESIGNING YOUR EXPERIMENT
Review the steps necessary to complete the design for the experiment in your textbook. Before you begin the experiment, use the space below to record the details of what you will be doing.

- Hypothesis: _____

_____

- Population to be studied: _____

_____

- Sample make-up: _____

_____

- Control group: _____

_____

- Experimental group: _____

_____

- Independent variable(s): _____

- Dependent variable(s): _____

- Variable(s) to remain constant: _____

- Potential confounding variable(s): _____

- Evidence of experimenter bias: _____

- Ethical concerns: _____

3. PRESENTING YOUR EXPERIMENTAL DESIGN

As you prepare to present your experiment to the class, use the table below
to make notes about concerns that are likely to come up after your
presentation.

Design	Sample/Population	Control	Ethics

What did your classmates suggest to improve your experimental design?
Write a brief description in the space below.

_____

_____

_____

_____

4. DISCUSSION

Discuss the strengths and weaknesses of the various experimental designs.
Then use the space below to write a brief description of a new design
incorporating what you have learned.

_____

_____

_____

_____